BE A NEURO-ADVOCATE

# BE A NEURO-ADVOCATE

## AN INTERSECTIONAL EXPLORATION OF NEUROLOGICAL DISEASES AND BRAIN-HEALTH ADVOCACY

MELODY A. CHANG

NEW DEGREE PRESS

COPYRIGHT © 2020 MELODY A. CHANG



BE A NEURO-ADVOCATE

*An Intersectional Exploration of Neurological Diseases and Brain-Health Advocacy*

ISBN      978-1-64137-399-9  *Paperback*

              978-1-64137-400-2  *Kindle Ebook*

              978-1-64137-401-9  *Ebook*

# CONTENTS

# ACKNOWLEDGMENTS

With gratitude, I thank those who have been involved in supporting me in this endeavor. Oftentimes, life throws opportunities at us that we ought to take regardless of whether we feel ready to or not. Publishing this book was one of those instances.

I am endlessly grateful to those who provided the direction to write this book. Thank you to Professor Eric Koester for reaching out. As for New Degree Press and Brian Bies, a large thank you as well. Finally, I have much appreciation for the publishing team who directly helped with editing in various ways, including Anthony Franklin, Bailee Noella, and Amanda Brown. The dedication to this particular book took a compilation of over 1,000 hours of my own and a similar amount from those on the publishing side.  Thank you to Cheryl Jacobs and Dr. John DenBoer for being willing to speak to a complete stranger on the relevant topics in the book. Cheers to your organizations making great strides!

As for the experiences that have shaped my ongoing perspectives on life, I am beyond blessed to have been given those opportunities and have individuals invested in fostering my growth. A huge shout-out to Dr. Larry Fan, Joey

Chang, Marissa McKool, Erin Schwartz, Lauren Dacorro, Marcela Rodriguez, Sumana Shashidar, Sue Swope, and Dr. Anzaldua.

As for my personal supporters of the book, I want to thank:

| | |
|---|---|
| Raymond Clubb | Venus Chou |
| Sophia Chang | Jeremie Kim |
| Tina Wang | Libby Kardontchik |
| Yamin Su | Ashley Bivens |
| Lee Yi Wang | Oliver Yeh |
| Wendy Huang | Albert Fang |
| Pengfei Dou | David Song |
| Hui-Lan Wen | Jack O'Reilly |
| John Tsai | Anthony Trias |
| James Crawford | Carol Liu |
| Sarah McCartin | Lee Thomas |
| Sigrid Fry-Revere | Karen Trejo |

and many more for your direct support throughout much of the journey. I truly hope you have individuals who are as incredible as these folks who root for you in all your undertakings.

# HOW TO NAVIGATE THIS BOOK

---

**IDENTIFY WHY YOU ARE READING THIS BOOK**

If you have picked up this book, thank you. There are several reasons why you may be reading, and all of them are valid and appreciated. For the curious reader with limited knowledge of brain health and diseases, I recommend reading the entire book. With that in mind, there are four major sections of the book, which can be navigated accordingly.

If you have limited knowledge of the history of the brain or brain health itself, I would point you directly to the Introduction. Part 1 contains the introduction and Chapter 1-2 on the history of the human brain and development. These chapters consider how current society approaches brain health and the misconceptions associated with the brain. Here, we examine the evolutionary history of the human brain, the early neuroscience research in the twentieth century, and human brain development with the perspective of neuroplasticity.

If you are primarily interested in the main sectors that interact with brain health such as research or medicine, navigate to Chapter 3. Part 2 contains Chapters 3–5. This portion of the book describes sectors that directly influence the brain, including public health, research, and medicine. Here, we uncover the history of major public health interventions for protecting brain health, as well as a secondary look into Dr. Eskenazi's life work in research on the effects of pesticides for brain health. For behavior-based research, I highlight research from world-renowned scientists, including Suzuki's research on exercise and Mosconi's research on diet for brain function.

If you already have a good understanding of what is discussed in Part 1 and Part 2, navigate to Part 3, which dives into brain diseases and health advocacy, specifically relating to each of the major brain diseases. Part 3 contains Chapters 6–10. In this section, we explore the primary issues in brain health, including traumatic brain injuries, brain cancer, neurological disorders, strokes, and dementia. In each of these chapters, I focus on humanizing the experiences of prominent individuals who have undergone brain health issues and the impact they hold around the brain health movement. For each major disease category, I delve into historical movements, prominent past and upcoming research, advocacy programs, and nonprofit organizations. One of the doctors interviewed on Alzheimer's and dementia released a Netflix documentary in 2019 and shared his story of how he was inspired to create his interventional program.

If you are looking for information surrounding the intersections of brain health and other novel sectors, including technology and media, I would point you to Chapter 11.

Part 4 contains Chapters 11–15 and the conclusion. In the final chapters of the book, I discuss the newest incorporations into brain health, including corporate wellness programs, upcoming pharmaceutical nootropics—also commonly termed as "smart drugs"—digital therapeutics, and social media movements. I found and highlighted stories from innovative individuals who aim to make strides for brain health, such as Adrian Gore, a South African billionaire, and Adam Gazzaley, a University of California, San Francisco physician and principal investigator of Neuroscape. In each of the chapters, I explore the idea of validity in interventions and examine how these new avenues may positively affect the future of our society in relation to brain health.

Each chapter takes on one specific story, tied to one major topic within brain health. As a result, each chapter can be read independently based on personal interest in the subject matter.

**TAKE ACTION**

More importantly than reading the entire book, I hope to provide you with ways to become larger than the reader of this book. The ultimate aim is for you to develop into the initiator, one who actually acts upon new knowledge gained. I have created suggestions that vary in specificity to certain individuals, so keep an eye open for those actionable items at the end of each chapter.

At the end of the day, whether it be taking ownership of your own brain health or contributing to the brain health advocacy movement, I am honored and grateful that you have chosen to read *Be a Neuro-Advocate*.

# CURIOSITY: THE START OF YOUR SEARCH FOR KNOWLEDGE

---

*"The wisest mind has something yet to learn."*

– GEORGE SANTAYANA [1]

"All of my mind equates to that?" I thought in disbelief as my neurobiology professor gently removed the human organ from its preservation case. It felt almost surreal, yet fascinating that every single one of my thoughts, the capacity of all of my comprehensive skills, who I believed I was, and who I wanted to be originated entirely from this one organ: the human brain.

---

1    "Even The Wisest Mind Has Something Yet To Learn."". 2020. *Passiton.Com.* https://www.passiton.com/inspirational-quotes/4024-even-the-wisest-mind-has-something-yet-to-learn.

As I cradled the human brain in my gloved hands, I fully recognized that most people would never have the opportunity to touch, let alone see, a real human brain in their lifetime. The more I pondered the thought, the more I wondered whether the general public would even be curious enough to explore the brain if given the chance in a learning setting. Initially, I found it incredulous that any single person might have zero curiosity about the brain.

When I walked back to my college apartment that same day, I relayed the story to my housemate about holding a human brain in the lab and asked, "How curious would you say you are about the brain?" Queasiness aside, she stated that the brain was undeniably something that sparked her curiosity, but that she had never taken any initiative to discover more. That night, I turned the statement over and over again in my head, wondering what exactly cultivates enough curiosity about the brain in an individual to take action to learn more.

Beyond that, is the general public motivated to discover more about their own brains and to what extent? Why is it that millennials are so much more aware of the influencers on Instagram or celebrities' every move yet have so little curiosity about the brain? Why is it that many of us, when referring to health, only consider the physical aspects of health without attending to our brain health? I believe that it narrows down to several overarching components.

## CURRENT STATE OF THE WORLD

Consider this: the American Heart Association claims three out of five Americans will develop a brain disease in their lifetime.[2] According to the World Health Organization, brain

---

2    "Brain Health". 2019. American Heart Association.

diseases and neurological disorders are a growing public health epidemic. In 2016, the Global Burden of Neurological Disorders study was conducted by the World Health Organization and the Harvard School of Public Health in an attempt to understand the global burden of neurological disorders.[3]

From many perspectives, whether that be as a numerical cost for society or as a personal concern for individual relationships, brain health matters. The study concluded that neurological disorders are the number one leading cause of Disability Adjusted Life Years (DALYs), a measure of disease burden that indicates a sum of years of potential life lost due to mortality and years of productive life lost due to disability. Moreover, over the last three decades, the burden of neurological disorders has increased and is predicted to increase with the aging of the population.[4] All of this research is leading toward an increasing global demand for resources that aid in brain disease prevention or resources that support brain health treatment and management.

Currently, our society holds these misconceptions about brain health:

A) Most individuals hold the misconception that learning about the brain is too difficult and not beneficial or worth the effort for personal well-being.

I find this to be the largest hurdle for most people to cross. Neurobiology and neuroscience are not topics that

3   Aarli, Johan, Taran Dua, Aleksandar Janca, and Anna Muscetta. 2008. "Neurological Disorders: Public Health Challenges". Archives Of Neurology 65 (1): 154. doi:10.1001/archneurol.2007.19.

4   Naghavi, Mohsen. 2019. "Global, Regional, And National Burden Of Suicide Mortality 1990 To 2016: Systematic Analysis For The Global Burden Of Disease Study 2016". BMJ, l94. doi:10.1136/bmj.l94.

are frequently explored in high school and rarely in college either, unless an individual decides to pursue neurobiology or neuroscience as their major. While the brain is fascinating, it is undeniably complicated. There are many ongoing research and clinical studies and many professionals who are engaged in continuing to develop our holistic understanding of brain mechanisms and functions.

However, it is beneficial for the average person to have an understanding of the brain with the intention of understanding how to care for their own brain. Obtaining basic knowledge allows one to engage in healthy behaviors that benefit or maintain the state of a cognitively sound brain.

According to the surveys conducted by the American Association of Retired Persons (AARP), more brain-healthy behaviors are correlated with better mental well-being scores. Along with that, adults who engage in mentally stimulating activities, such as learning new things or reading books, also have higher mental well-being.[5] Though we may have heard these facts before, there is more to explore within the realm of brain health. In order to challenge our current knowledge, it is important to turn the question around and ask ourselves what we do not know.

For example, do we know the symptoms and risks of a stroke or a traumatic brain injury in case it ever happens to us? Are we aware of how to ensure our child develops cognitively within the first five years of life? Are we up to date about the new technology in the field of brain health that has the most potential to impact Alzheimer's? There is so much to learn about the brain, and there is bound to

5    Skufca, Laura. 2015 Survey on Brain Health. Washington, DC: AARP Research, October 2015.

be a subject that interests you, whether it be neurological diseases or neuroimaging or brain development. The list is endless. In order to foster our knowledge, it is essential to first and foremost recognize that we all depend so heavily on the brain for every single action or thought. The information you encounter about the brain will in some way, shape, or form be relevant to you. Let's not take our brains for granted.

B) The general public values and pays much more attention to physical health and fitness compared to brain health.

Since 2010, there has been a major movement in physical health and fitness. Social media has granted us eternal access to outlets of "fitspiration" and motivational influencers who promote healthy eating and habitual exercise. I myself jumped on the train at the beginning of my college career and currently follow many fitness YouTubers and Instagram accounts that motivate my desire to continue a healthy physical lifestyle.

As a nation, we have long recognized that physical health is a major issue, and over the last few decades, there have been many movements that attempt to address the issue. On the official website of the U.S. Department of Health and Human Services, the "Resource Center" page lists all the organizations that offer credible resources on physical activity, such as the Move Your Way Campaign or Go4Life campaign.[6] People from the President's Council on Sports, Fitness, and Nutrition tweet reminders like "Movement is life!! These 'super seniors' are living longer, healthier lives."[7] The population as a whole understands the value of physical

6   "Physical Activity Resources". 2019. HHS.Gov.

7   "President's Council On Sports, Fitness & Nutrition (PCSFN)". 2019. HHS.Gov.

exercise. Do we as a population hold brain health to the same degree of importance?

Another survey from 2015 under AARP examined how important brain health is for more than 1,500 adults over the age of forty. Around 83 percent of adults surveyed indicated that maintaining or improving brain health was very important from their personal perspective. Around 73 percent noted concern about declining brain health in the future.[8] However, there is a notable discrepancy between the high numbers of people who recognize the importance of brain health compared to the percentage of people who actually engage in healthy brain behaviors. AARP suggested that increasing knowledge may directly correlate to engaging in healthier brain behaviors. As stated by Sarah Lenz Lock, a senior vice president of AARP, "This new survey is showing that there are big gaps between what people think is important for their brains and what they are actually doing to maintain their brain health." [9]

C) There is perhaps a lack of advocacy and not enough accurate social movement has been generated for brain health.

In the past decades prior to the era of the Internet, information has been disseminated primarily directly from medical professionals. However, according to a survey performed in Canada, 70 percent of individuals view

---

8    Skufca, Laura. 2015 Survey on Brain Health. Washington, DC: AARP Research, October 2015.

9    Agnvall, Elizabeth. 2019. "New Survey: Americans Say Brain Health Is Crucial, But Protection Is Challenging". Blog: American Association Of Retired Persons.

the internet as their first source of health-related information.[10] While the accessibility of information has evidently increased as a result, inherent difficulties include regulation and quality control of the health literature promoted. As witnessed by the large anti-vaxxer groups on social media that spread inaccurate information on Facebook and other platforms in 2018, the consequences of buying into false messages can be dangerous.

I am suggesting a shift back to looking to medical and health professionals for accurate information. Due to the shifting cultural paradigm of reliance on the web as a resource, it is important for people within the professional community to speak up and let their voices be heard in different ways. There has been a bit of media coverage and attention on the subject of brain health. The organizations that accurately and actively disseminate information are inspiring and should be the standard.

The other factor in professional advocacy is garnering interest in the upcoming technological developments, research, and movements in brain health. This should not be a topic that people neglect until they turn sixty-five and then suddenly begin fretting about what brain health entails. Instead, attention to brain health should be fostered in generations starting at a young age. Promoting advocacy for brain health or fostering movements that focus on brain health advocacy is one method of increasing engagement.

---

10   Tonsaker, Tabitha. 2016. "Gold Mine Or Minefield?". New Scientist 231 (3084): 5. doi:10.1016/s0262-4079(16)31341-0.

**I believe**

- Brain health is becoming an issue that needs to be discussed due to the increase in neurological diseases related to an aging population
- Research and information are not actually disseminated well, and changes that improve brain health are not addressed quickly enough

While I was an intern at UCSF's Memory and Aging Center, I worked primarily with adults over the age of sixty-five. Despite being aware that neurological disorders are deemed as one of the top-growing global burdens as defined by the World Health Organization, I did not fully consider the implications. While conducting neuropsychological examinations to evaluate cognition and memory, it became evident to me that cognitive decline was truly happening in the aging population on a global aggregate scale. A large majority of people in our society have not been and do not actively take care of their minds in the way we should.

Then, in interacting with individuals in my generation as well, it was clear that most of my peers did not care much at all about brain or neurological health. I asked myself: how do I get a whole generation of individuals to care about their brains? In my book, I focus on framing research, medicine, and diseases in a way that may directly reach those who inaccurately assume brain health has no relevance to them. Along with that, I aim to spark continued conversation and curiosity by introducing new technology, therapeutics, and ideas for brain health advocacy.

My hope is that, in reading this book, you will discover how each and every one of you plays a vital role in the movement of brain health advocacy, whether your efforts are directed toward yourself or toward society as a whole. In this book, I hope to instill the same sort of passion and curiosity I have for neuroscience and brain health advocacy in you. Ultimately, I want you to see this book as a tool to help you take ownership of your own neurological and cognitive well-being and how you can shape the brain health movement.

Throughout the entirety of the book, I aim to incorporate you into primary parts of my world as I relay my perspective on my meaningful experiences, from studying neurobiology at the University of California, Berkeley to volunteering in a public health nonprofit in Ghana to having my first glance in research at a UCSF neuroscience lab to interning at and understanding the environment of the pharmaceutical industry to immersing myself in clinical research to wholly empathizing with what it entails to lose loved ones to a major disease, and how each of these experiences has contributed to my mission of understanding every sector that largely influences brain health and comprehending all angles on brain health advocacy.

### Who is this For?
- People who have curious minds and want to learn more about the current status of the brain health industry and what is to come
- People who are into neurology, neuropsychology, and neuroscience and want to hear interesting perspectives
- People who enjoy health advocacy, whether that be health professionals or nonprofit organizations

### Why Read It?
- Dr. John DenBoer, who received training at the VA Boston Healthcare System as a clinical neuropsychologist,

and his heartfelt story of how he was inspired to create early-dementia interventional programs. DenBoer is the founder, CEO, and chief medical officer of SMART Brain Aging and has his own highly rated Netflix documentary that was released in 2019 called *This Is Dementia*.

- The Vitality Group, Inc., a global research organization that takes action for health promotion and chronic disease prevention and aims in fostering a healthy diet, physical activity, avoidance of tobacco and alcohol, medication adherence, and mental health. Here, we hear from The Vitality Group about how CEO Adrian Gore, a South African billionaire and entrepreneur of Discovery Limited, founded Vitality's relationship with the Apple Watch. More specifically, we discover how wellness programs can make a significant impact in all areas of health, including mental well-being.

- Communicating published research surrounding brain health, with ideas backed up by world-renowned researchers and physicians, and relating these directly back to how we can take ownership of our brain health.

- Incorporating the journeys of individuals who have undergone brain injuries or diseases with how they have overcome adversities and made a lasting impact in the realm of health advocacy and methods that we can become further involved in creating large-scale change.

In this book, we examine the historical and cultural aspects of brain health. We will be exploring several exemplary professionals who have dedicated their lives to brain health, research, and advocacy. Within brain health movements, I will illustrate the differences between evidence-based research and consumer-based brain health products that have not proven to hold true value. Along with that, I aim to foster interest by highlighting the recent and potential developments in the realm of brain health. As a final aim, I hope to empower individuals like yourself to be diligent and proactive about your journey with your own brain.

# PART I

# THE BRAIN BASICS: AN EVOLUTIONARY AND DEVELOPMENTAL PERSPECTIVE ON THE BRAIN

# CHAPTER 1

# THE MODERN RELATIONSHIP OF HUMANITY AND THE BRAIN

—

*"The human brain is probably one of the most complex single objects on the face of the earth; I think it is, quite honestly."*

–BILL VIOLA [11]

"What do you guys think evolved first: the modern human brain or the bipedal upright walking?" my professor asked the class. I sat there, realizing for the first time that I knew close to nothing about the evolutionary history of the human brain. While I had heard of Lucy and the hominids that had evolved before Homo sapiens, I was dutifully aware that

---

11    "Bill Viola Quotes". 2019. Brainyquote.

I lacked familiarity with human brain evolution. As each slide detailed the approximate brain size for each hominid, I was intimidated by all the numbers I had to memorize but simultaneously excited to be delving into a new ground of brain territory.

Within my years at Berkeley, the specific courses detailing brain anatomy and evolution in relation to the brain were the most challenging subjects to grasp. The topic of brain evolution has become the primary career focus of many individuals throughout the anthropological and biological fields, and the learning is extensive, to say the least. Here, we will dive into the evolutionary perspective and the advancement of tools we use to study the human brain.

## WHAT IS REVEALED ABOUT OUR BRAIN EVOLUTION?

Have you ever wondered how we gather information from the brains of fossils? Brains are organs that do not fossilize, and instead, as they deteriorate, a cavity is left inside the brain known as the braincase. Scientists most often use artificial endocasts in order to study the accurate measurement of brain size. Traditionally, the endocasts are made of rubber material, but in recent years, scientists have been using Computed Tomography (CT) scanning technology to create digital endocasts. Endocasts are replicas of early and modern human braincases. When endocasts are created, they are close in size and shape to the former brains that occupied the braincases. [12]

Endocasts of hominids have been used to determine an estimate of brain sizes across the evolutionary timeline. From

_______________

12   "Ardipithecus Ramidus". 2019. The Smithsonian Institution's Human Origins Program.

1992 to 1993, the Berkeley professor Tim White discovered the bones of *Ardipithecus ramidus* in the Middle Awash river valley in Ethiopia. It took a total sum of around seventeen entire years to reconstruct and analyze the skeletons of *Ardipithecus ramidus*. Ardi was interpreted to be a four-foot-tall female specimen and the fossils were dated at least to around 4.4 million years ago. Ardi's endocast had a small brain size of around 300 to 350 cubic centimeters. For reference, the size of the *A. radimus* brain was a little smaller than that of a modern-day female chimpanzee. [13]

A few decades earlier, Lucy was found by Donald Johanson and Tom Gray at the Ethiopian site of Hadar. Johnson and Gray were both famous anthropologists and professors in anthropology. On November 24, 1974, Johanson and Gray were traveling over the site of Hadar, just about to end a day's work of surveying for fossils. Taking an alternate route back to the Land Rover, Johanson spotted a white, gleaming object and quickly identified it to be the right proximal ulna of a hominid. The right proximal ulna is also known as the forearm bone. To their luck, the search did not end there. Instead, the pair found an extensive collection of fossils including the occipital skull bone, femur, ribs, pelvis, and lower jaw. That November night, Johanson and Gray celebrated the excitement of finding a new hominid, and the Beatles' song, "Lucy in the Sky with Diamonds" played in the background over and over. The name Lucy stuck and it took about two more weeks to fully excavate 40 percent of the hominid skeleton. [14]

---

13  "04.12.2006 - Ethiopian Fossils Link Ape-Men With Earlier Hominids". 2019. Berkeley.Edu.

14  "Tim D. White | American Paleoanthropologist". 2019. Encyclopedia Britannica.

Lucy, an *Australopithecus afarensis* fossil, is one of the oldest fossils in forensic history, dating to around three million years ago. The *Australopithecus afarensis* was one of the first hominids deemed bipedal, capable of walking on two limbs. Lucy's species had a brain size of around 400 to 550 cc. The trend for hominid brains throughout evolution was exampled in these species as a trajectory of increasing brain sizes.

For the *Homo habilis*, the first stone toolmakers who lived between 2.1 and 1.5 million years ago, there was a notable expansion in the brain size. The *Homo habilis* was discovered in the 1960s by Louis and Mary Leaky, who uncovered the fossils in Tanzania. With a brain size of around 550 to 687 cc, the neocortex and frontal lobe had both expanded significantly compared to earlier species. [15]

Neocortex—the part of the mammalian brain that is involved in sensory processing, cognition, motor commands, language

Frontal Lobe—part of the brain that controls executive functions including communication, consciousness, memory, attention

There were several species following the *Homo habilis*. Around 1.8 million years ago, the species Homo erectus existed with a brain size of over 850 to 1100 cc. The growth of the hominid brain size from this point out is considered to be exponential. *Homo Neanderthals* and *Homo sapiens* both had cranial capacities averaging around 1,200 to 1,600 cc. *Homo neanderthals* are the closest extinct relatives that lived in Eurasia approximately 200,000 to 30,000 years ago.

---

15   @ErinWayman, Follow. 2019. "Louis Leakey: The Father Of Hominid Hunting". Smithsonian.

They were known to have overlapping existence with *Homo sapiens*, which is the human species. As stated by Antonio Rosas, chairman of the paleoanthropology group at Spain's National Museum of Natural Sciences in Madrid, "It took a little bit longer for the brain to grow in Neanderthals than in modern humans. What we realize now is that this pattern of slow growth that allows us to have this big brain and mature slowly, with all the advantages involved with that, was also shared by different human species." [16] In evolutionary history, the larger brain sizes simultaneously had a strong positive correlation with social group size as nuclear families became more common with a larger brain size.

Today, the average brain size can be measured by magnetic resonance imaging (MRI) scans for volume. For modern human brain sizes, the average adult brain volume is around 1,260 ccs for men and 1,130 ccs for women, with a fairly large degree of variation. At birth, however, humans are born much more neurologically immature than other primates. Other primates, such as macaque monkeys, are born with 70 percent of adult brain size. After the nine-month gestation, human babies are born with less than 30 percent of the adult brain size. In order for our ancestors to have obtained the evolutionary benefits of bipedal walking, the hip sizes of women were slightly smaller in angle than that of prior species within our lineage. While it seems counterintuitive that human babies are born with such neurologically immature brains, in evolutionary biology, this is termed as an evolutionary tradeoff, which enabled bipedal walking and a smaller average brain at birth for babies of

---

16  Choi, Charles. 2019. "How Neanderthals Got Their Unusually Large Brains". Livescience.Com.

our species. While the anthropology of the brain is one realm that was extremely well-explored in the late 1900s, the research around the brain in the early 1990s was highly focused on deriving tools for electrical brain recordings, neuroimaging, and understanding the basic functions of different parts of the brain.[17]

## TECHNIQUES MEASURING THE MODERN BRAIN

In the mid-1920s, Hans Berger obtained the first recordings of human electrical brain waves in the form of electroencephalograms (EEG). As neurologist David Millett wrote, "These first recordings of the human EEG are remarkably unimpressive: coarse shadows of minute oscillations on the galvanometer string captured on photographic paper." [18] Slowly, in upcoming years, Berger began refining the process to create more legible EEGs. After years of attempts, 73 EEGs on his own son and 56 on himself, Berger developed the standard EEG we know today. Today, EEGs are important for determining the electrical activity of the brain and used in modern medicine to monitor seizures and evaluate brain activity after head injuries.

Around the same period, in 1927, Egas Moniz began introducing the idea of neuroimaging through a method known as cerebral angiography. Angiography, however, allows visualization inside blood vessels but had long-term risks when

17    Hofman, Michel A. 2014. "Evolution Of The Human Brain: When Bigger Is Better". Frontiers In Neuroanatomy 8. doi:10.3389/fnana.2014.00015.

18    Laskow, Sarah. 2019. "The Role Of The Supernatural In The Discovery Of Eegs". The Atlantic.

utilized for the brain. [19] Over the course of several decades in the twentieth century, angiographies were refined to be safe for the patients involved. For neurosurgeons today, angiographies are commonly used for imaging cerebral aneurysms and blood-vessel lesions.

By the mid-twentieth century, the great strides surrounding brain research continued to surround developing tools for neurology. By 1963, the idea of a computed tomography scan was finally successfully developed by Dr. William Oldendorf, a University of California, Los Angeles neurologist. Oldendorf spent two years developing the prototype from scratch after his initial inspiration came directly from apparatus that scanned fruit and rejected the fruit that had dehydrated portions. In 1971, Sir Godfrey Hounsfield took the model and developed the first commercial version of the CT scanner. Today, CT scans are conventionally used to detect head injuries, strokes, and brain tumors in a noninvasive manner.

The last of the main neuroimaging techniques developed was the MRI. After the CT scan was successfully commercialized, researchers wanted to determine if there was another way to create images without radiation. Magnetic fields and protons came into conversation as an alternative method. Protons, positively charged particles in all atoms, align when placed in a strong magnetic field. Once a radiofrequency current is sent through the patient, these positive protons are stimulated and strain against the magnetic field.

---

19   Artico, Marco, Marialuisa Spoletini, Lorenzo Fumagalli, Francesca Biagioni, Larisa Ryskalin, Francesco Fornai, Maurizio Salvati, Alessandro Frati, Francesco Saverio Pastore, and Samanta Taurone. 2017. "Egas Moniz: 90 Years (1927–2017) From Cerebral Angiography". Frontiers In Neuroanatomy 11. doi:10.3389/fnana.2017.00081.

As the positive protons realign with the magnetic field, MRI sensors can then detect the amount of energy released. After years of research for the MRI during the 1980s, Paul Lauterbur and Sir Peter Mansfield were granted the 2003 Nobel Prize in Physiology or Medicine.

**LIST OF BRAIN IMAGING TECHNOLOGY:**

Electroencephalogram (EEG)—using small electrodes attached to the scalp, the EEG can test electrical activity in the brain. Brain cells communicate through impulses termed as brain waves. Each electrode is connected to an EEG recording machine.

Angiography—an X-ray that detects blockages in arteries. It requires injecting iodine dye as a contrasting substance for visualization.

Computed Tomography Scan (CT)—using a series of X-ray images taken at multiple angles around the body, the computer processor will combine the images to create cross-sectional images of the body. This produces better images than normal X-rays.

Structural MRI—Structural MRIs can differentiate between white matter and gray matter of the brain and can also detect tumors and aneurysms. Because there is no radiation associated with MRIs, it is often the choice used when performing brain scans.

Functional MRI—detects changes in blood flow in the brain. The activated brain structures utilize more oxygen and therefore, fMRI requires a blood oxygen level-dependent contrast. When an area of the brain is activated, more cerebral blood flow occurs in that specific region of the brain.

## ADVOCACY FOR UNDERSTANDING THE BRAIN

As evidenced by the history above, most of the common techniques utilized in neurology were developed on a relatively short timeline. Similarly, the understanding of the brain has dramatically increased since the late twentieth century as a result of the efforts of numerous curious researchers. Starting in 1907, the research by Santiago Ramón y Cajal was one of the first in the cascade of discoveries that followed. Ramón y Cajal initiated the neuron doctrine, which outlined the nervous system as discrete individual cells known as neurons. [20]

From the 1920s to the 1950s, many experiments were performed on mice to better understand the functionalities of distinct brain regions. In 1929, Karl Lashley used lesion experiments in mice to find the region of the brain responsible for memory. Similarly, Wilder Penfield and Theodore Rasmussen were both successful in mapping the motor and sensory regions of the brain. In similar manners, many different areas of the brain were shown to correspond to specific functions. By 1952, the detailed synaptic transmissions between neurons were illustrated by Sir Alan Hogdkin and Sir Andrew Huxley, depicting an accurate snapshot of how neurons communicate to form neural connections. All of these were essential additions to the modern view of how we perceive the human brain. [21]

In the 1980s, the Society for Neuroscience dedicated its efforts to lobbying in Congress for increased funding for neuroscience. The Society for Neuroscience, along with the National Committee for Research in Neurological and

---

20 "Cajal". 2019. Psu.Edu.

21 Marshall, Louise H, and Horace Winchell Magoun. 2010. Discoveries In The Human Brain. Totowa, N.J.: Humana Press.

Communicative Disorders (NCRCD) corresponded with legislators in Washington, DC. By 1987, the lobbyists had generated enough buy-in from Congress to advance funding for neuroscience in both research and clinical development. The years from 1990 to 1999 were the "Decade of the Brain," as proposed under the presidency of George Bush. The initiative was designated by Congress, proclaiming "a new era of discovery dawning in brain research." [22]

By 1992, meetings and lectures were held consistently to discuss the aims of the research. Sixty scientists signed a formal declaration listing ten research aims to be accomplished by 2000. This declaration stimulated other international communities to participate in the large-scale movement, including Japan, whose government invested $125 million in neuroscience research by 1997. [23] Likewise, China and India founded neuroscience institutes around the same time.

According to Dr. Lewis P. Rowland, an American neurologist, "As a way of engaging scientists, legislators, and leaders of voluntary agencies, it was a success. As an education program, it successfully mirrored the wonderful scientific and technological advances." [24] The most notable developments during the decade were the development of fMRI, the discovery of neural plasticity and understanding of neural

---

22  "Sfn Expands Advocacy Efforts To Amplify Need For Funding"" 2019. Sfn.Org.

23  Habermann, Barbara. 2001. "Decade Of Behavior Follows The Decade Of The Brain". Journal Of Neuroscience Nursing 33 (2): 117. doi:10.1097/01376517-200104000-00011.

24  Rowland, Lewis P. 2003. NINDS At 50. New York: Demos Medical Pub., LLC.

development, the understandings of several genes responsible for brain diseases such as Huntington's Disease, and the societal recognition of the importance of early experiences on a child's brain development. The Dana Foundation, one of the main public journals covering neuroscience research, released a commentary surrounding the Decade of the Brain in 2010. [25]

Until the Decade of the Brain, the adult brain was seen as static and not very malleable. However, neuroscientists have found that to be widely incorrect and instead, this suggests the brain is malleable and changing. At all ages, the brain is responsive to environmental stimuli, and the connections within the brain are dynamic. Neuroplasticity is modulated by both genetic and epigenetic processes. Moreover, there is current evidence pointing to social stimuli as a source of influence on the human brain and that social experiences can modify the epigenetics of the brain as well.

The Decade of the Brain research also uncovered new drug and behavioral treatments for mental disorders. Mental disorders, prior to the 1990s, were not predominantly viewed as brain disorders. As a result of research that quantified differences in neurotransmitter levels in the brain as a correlation to specific mental disorders, these disorders were reclassified as brain-related. Researchers in this decade were then able to determine that several of the brain disorders were circuit-based. As a result, the manner in which medical professionals and researchers approach disorders relating to the brain has changed drastically. Disorders such as depression and schizophrenia are currently

---

25  "DANA Foundation". 2019. Dana.Org.

being researched as disruptions in brain circuitry during development.

Along with that, research during the Decade of the Brain showed that genetic defects correlate to certain brain disorders and rare diseases. For example, there are fifteen identified genes that directly cause spinocerebellar ataxia. Separate gene mutations were found to be a cause of Huntington's disease, Amyotrophic lateral sclerosis, and Rett syndrome. Although identification was the very first step in understanding the mechanisms for certain diseases, the translation process of scientific knowledge to treatments has proven to be difficult. Overall, while the Decade of the Brain was successful in unraveling many of the mysteries of the brain, it raised more questions than it answered. [26]

**FUTURE-FORWARD:**

Twenty-five years later, according to Dr. Jason Campagna, the senior vice president of Health Sciences Leads, many of the questions entering the Decade of the Brain remain unsolved. As an example, what is consciousness? How do we prevent Alzheimer's or strokes? Regardless of the excitement, the buzz around the brain has slowed down. As Campagna states, "Back in 1995, when *Science* featured a cover showcasing the 'Decade of the Brain,' I thought in 2015 we'd have stroke treatments which, like heart attack care today, allow people to essentially walk out of a hospital after a needle stick and wire to place a stent." [27] Although

---

26  "Decade Of The Brain Home Page (Library Of Congress)". 2019. Loc.Gov.

27  "Xconomy: The Decade Of The Brain: 25 Years Later". 2019. Xconomy.

it has only been two decades since the Decade of the Brain, individuals in Generation Z are unlikely to remember or recall this proposal.

### Decade of the Mind

Unbeknownst to many, we are currently in the middle of the "Decade of the Mind." This project is an international initiative also aimed at advancing the understanding of the mind in relation to the brain. The initiative was proposed for $4 billion and is supposed to span from 2012 to 2022. The top neuroscientists in the world—including James Albus, George Bekey, John Holland, Nancy Kanwisher, Jeffrey Krichmar, Mortimer Mishkin, Dharmendra Modha, Marcus Raichle, Gordon Shepherd, and Giulio Tononi—were involved in this proposal and published the movement in the *Science* journal. [28]

This initiative involves the growing research on brain diseases and mental disorders, especially the translational aspects of improving outcomes for those affected by them. What does it mean to be human and have a notion of self, rational thought processes, language, and higher consciousness?

How can we improve the outcomes in education and apply neuroscience research to those people between ages five and twenty to improve education? The ability to model the mind through analytical methods or computerized tools may produce new ways of developing hypotheses and research. From the first meeting to discuss the project in 2007, the focus has been on five broad initiatives:

---

28  Spitzer, Manfred. 2008. "Decade Of The Mind". Philosophy, Ethics, And Humanities In Medicine 3 (1): 7. doi:10.1186/1747-5341-3-7.

A. Understanding the Brain

B. Healing and Protecting the Brain

C. Enriching the Mind

D. Building Artificial Models of the Brain

E. Improving Public Knowledge of the Brain

What does this mean for those of us, perhaps, not involved in the professional research community?

As seen in the Decade of the Brain, this project was a collaborative effort not just of research professionals but also of lobbyists, politicians, nonprofit organization staff members, administrators, public relations professionals, news reporters, and more. The last century has been incredible for brain research in understanding the evolutionary development of the human brain, in piloting new neuroscience tools, and in modifying some of the fundamental understandings of the human brain. May we, as a new generation, hunger for that same level of knowledge?

**Actionable Ideas:**

1. Which of the objectives above from the Decade of the Mind resonates most with you? Which of these do you feel like you can potentially have some form of positive influence on?

2. What are you most curious about within this introduction? Is it anthropology in relation to the brain, techniques used to understand the brain or policy movements for brain research? As you can see, there are a lot of intersections between understanding and engaging with the mind. We'll collaboratively aim to determine what roles you can play and what niches you can hold in the brain sector.

*As White stated in an interview, "The human species is a very unusual mammal, it turns out. We have very large brains. We have a unique way of walking around—two legs. And we would like to know how that happened. We have a technology that is overwhelming—in fact, it's threatening the planet today. We would like to know how that happened." [29]*

---

29 "Conversation With Tim White, P. 2 Of 6". 2019. Globetrotter. Berkeley.Edu.

# THE IMPACT OF THE FIRST FIVE YEARS AND THE INEQUITY IN BRAIN GROWTH

---

*"The brain has a quality referred to as plasticity. The ability to form new neural pathways even into very old age. The brain is fluid, flexible and incredibly adaptable to new experiences."*

—DEEPAK CHOPRA[30]

In the early 1990s, my dad followed the trend of the Silicon Valley boom and emigrated from Taiwan to study at Oregon State and to later work in the tech industry. Feeling

---

30  "Deepak Chopra Quote: 'The Brain Has A Quality Referred To As Plasticity. The Ability To Form New Neural Pathways Even Into Very Old Age. The B...'". 2019. Quotefancy.Com.

lucky to be in the States, my mother found herself in the heart of San Jose at the age of twenty-five after marrying my father. In September 1993, she gave birth to my older sister, Sophia.

Given that my mother worked a full-time job in accounting and my father worked full-time as an engineer, the only foreseeable option at the time was to send my sister to a full-time nanny. As Sophia began approaching the age of one, my mom noticed she was still primarily crawling instead of even trying to walk. In attempts to dig deeper into the issue, my mom discovered Sophia had been strapped into a baby chair every day at the nanny's and was simply stuck in front of a television for hours on end. It was an environment with no positive stimulation for Sophia, and she pulled my sister out of that nanny's house immediately. My mother began providing my sister with significantly more attention, despite having to balance a full-time job at the same time.

Three and a half years later, in April 1997, my mother gave birth to me. At this point in my parents' lives, they were living relatively comfortably and had bought their first house in Campbell, California. The moment my mother knew for sure that she was successfully in the prenatal third trimester, she made the decision to switch to a part-time job. Her main motivation in doing so was to make sure I grew up in a stimulating environment that fostered the normal stages of early development.

When I could not grasp the alphabet at the age of two, my mother spent significant time going through lessons with me on phonetics and, eventually, reading. My earliest memories, at around four or so, involved walking to the library with my sister and wheeling back as many books as our huge wagons and tote bags could carry. On a weekly basis, my sister and I indulged in endless amounts of solo reading. As an unspoken rule, we were limited to one single movie per week every Saturday night and never engaged in other television time during the ages of four through eighteen. Instead, our parents placed my sister and me in piano lessons and music classes starting at age three. Our parents also placed us in math development programs when I turned five to help foster logic-based skills. From five and up, my childhood involved activities such as swimming classes, art lessons, violin lessons, ice skating lessons, dance classes, professional choirs, summer programs, and church. I look back at every single opportunity I was provided with and cannot be more grateful. How did I get so lucky? I ask myself that every waking moment.

While I grew up believing my parents were strict beyond compare, I now understand they were creating environments in which we could be properly challenged and opportunities in which our minds flourished. Although I was born into an environment that was highly beneficial to brain development, many children are not given opportunities nearly to the extent I was in my childhood. I never for a second want to take what I have for granted.

When I lost my father in high school, I finally understood the degree of how blessed I was before, and for the first time in my life, I faced what it entailed to create opportunities for myself instead of being handed everything. Even more importantly, I encountered some of my best friends in college who were raised in settings opposite of mine. I admire each of them so much more knowing precisely all they overcame through life to attend Berkeley, in seeing their talents and in realizing the monumental accomplishments they built for themselves from scratch.

Health equity matters, and we as a society should be equally attentive to brain health equity. The system we live in is inherently unfair and unequal. We all start at different points in this journey of life, and we are all dealt with varying blessings and shortcomings. How can we adjust the system so we can truly give each child a more equal footing, especially for early brain development?

It turns out the human brain revolves around a plasticity that responds highly to the environment and to external interactions. Neuroplasticity, in simplistic terms, is the capacity for connections within the neurons to be altered through environmental and experiential input. There are two primary methods within neurobiology through which synaptic connections are altered: long-term potentiation and long-term depression. Long-term potentiation (LTP) strengthens the connections between two neurons, while long-term depression (LTD) weakens the connections between two neurons. The strengthening of connections or the weakening of connections creates familiar patterns that affect neural responses and pathways. In the larger picture, these patterns affect every aspect of the brain, from encoding new information to memory to learning and more. Research shows that neuroplasticity expands across the entire lifespan, as individual neurons are often responding to input that serve to increase LTP or LTD. However, with that in mind, there are specific periods in life in which the brain has much more neuroplasticity.

One million new neural connections are formed in each second of the first few years of life. From ages zero to five, our brains have the most plasticity to be influenced by changes in our environment. As the brain matures, research shows that plasticity decreases. Eighty percent of the child's brain develops by age three and 90 percent of the child's brain develops by age five. Therefore, between ages zero and five the architecture of the brain is extremely susceptible to change, and the right environment and stimulation are necessary for proper neural development.[31]

One of the key figures who illustrated environmentally based neuroplasticity through her research was Marian Diamond. In her lifetime, she became known as a pioneer in the field of neuroscience. Diamond grew up in Glendale, a city in Southern California, and was born to a father who was a physician and a mother who was a scholar of classics. At a young age, Marian's role models included Sir William Osler, a well-known physician and a family friend.

Marian knew very well that pursuing the sciences as a woman in the '60s was still an uphill battle. She often recalled the words of her family friend, Ben Sharpsteen, a Disney art director. "And he said, 'Someday, you'll be somebody.' Whenever life got tough, I remembered what he'd told me. So I had phenomenal role models, and when I met people that I didn't admire and they gave me a bad time, I just felt sorry for them, because I knew that I had grown up with really phenomenal people." [32]

By the early 1960s, Diamond was recruited to become an instructor at Cornell University. By 1984, Diamond's initial claim to fame as a neuroscientist came when preserved slices of Einstein's brain were sent for her to study. Her team analyzed the autopsy of Einstein's brain cortices in attempts to determine what made his intellect

---

31  "Brain Development - First Things First" 2019. First Things First.

32  Ranpura, Ashish. 2019. "A Conversation With Marian Diamond - Brain Connection". Brain Connection.

so outstanding. Despite the critics on her research surrounding Einstein, Diamond is most famously credited for making significant contributions to the fundamental concepts surrounding neuroplasticity. Contrary to the initial beliefs about the static nature of the brain, Diamond demonstrated that the structural and anatomical components of the physical brain could be altered by environmental factors.

## DISCOVERIES SURROUNDING NEUROPLASTICITY

As she began blossoming in science, Diamond became a professor of Integrative Biology at the University of California-Berkeley. Already, she was a mother of three and was successful in juggling her career and her family life. Within her research career, she made incredible strides.

Diamond's famous experiment involved altering the environments of rats to be either enriched or impoverished in the early stages of life. In Diamond's experiments, the enriched environments contained toys and companions in the rat cages, unlike the impoverished environments in which rats were isolated. The rats in impoverished environments demonstrated a significantly lower capacity to learn. In a maze experiment, rats with enriched environments had much more success navigating mazes than did rats that were isolated. The enriched rats also had a much thicker cerebral cortex structurally compared to impoverished rats. The cerebral cortex is a thin layer of the brain that is responsible for motor function, processing sensory information, language processing, planning and organization, personality, and intelligence. Beyond that, Diamond's research brought forth the idea that brain plasticity was viable throughout almost all of the lifespan, regardless of age or supposed brain growth periods. [33]

Following her accomplishments and successes within the research world, Diamond then created the Each One Teach One program for the school district in Albany. This program involved undergraduate mentors from the program teaching anatomy to students in kindergarten through eighth grade. The students were then highly encouraged to teach their parents what they learned in relation to anatomy. Dr. Diamond was equally encouraged by her research findings in the lab and was motivated to implement changes in the community around her.

## THE BABY BRAINIACS

Over the course of the last few decades, more research shows that, although brain plasticity occurs through the entirety of life, neuroplasticity has a clear age-dependent determinant. As human babies are born neurologically immature, it is estimated that the brain does not finish fully developing until age twenty-one for women and twenty-five for men. These estimates were standardized based on MRI-data that was focused on tracking the prefrontal cortex of the brain yearly for maturation and approximate end of growth. However, the most notable brain plasticity occurs when the immature brain is just beginning to develop by processing and engaging with sensory information. As a

---

33    Kentner, Amanda C., Kelly G. Lambert, Anthony J. Hannan, and S. Tifffany Donaldson. 2019. "Editorial: Environmental Enrichment: Enhancing Neural Plasticity, Resilience, And Repair". Frontiers In Behavioral Neuroscience 13. doi:10.3389/fnbeh.2019.00075.

result, infant's brains are extremely vulnerable to the environments they are placed in.

At the University of California-Berkeley, scientists scanned the brains of eighty-seven healthy babies from birth to around three months old. The most rapid change occurred with a growth of one percent average per day immediately after birth while the growth period slowed to around 0.4 percent growth per day by ninety days. Although the exact accuracy of the study may need to be validated through repetition, it reiterates just how important the early involvement and interactions are for proper brain development in children. [34]

Within year one, the cerebellum of the brain triples in size, allowing for increased motor control and enabling the visual areas of the cortex to develop into functional vision as well. At around three months, significant growth begins in the hippocampus, an area that relates to memory and recognition. Within year two, most of the changes occur in the language cognition regions of the brain, which correlates with development in the frontal and temporal lobes. The timeline of brain development corresponds with the child's vocabulary development and the infant starts to become more conscious and self-aware. In year three, the changes in the brain are predominantly within the prefrontal cortex, which is involved in cognitive flexibility and executive function. [35]

---

34   "Adolescent Development Research And Its Impact On Health Policy".
      2019. Unicef-Irc.Org.

35   Hodel, Amanda S. 2018. "Rapid Infant Prefrontal Cortex Development And Sensitivity To Early Environmental Experience". Developmental Review 48: 113-144. doi:10.1016/j.dr.2018.02.003.

## ENVIRONMENTS FOR POSITIVE BRAIN STIMULATION

The California Childcare Health Program suggested a few tips to help stimulate an infant's brain. All of these ideas can be used to create an interesting and engaging environment for infants:[36]

- Talking and singing to the infant
- Responding to the infant's requests
- Holding the infant
- Encouraging imitation
- Allowing the infant to explore
- Reading books to the infant
- Playing music

On the flip side, scientists have determined that toxic stress can also lead to changes in the architecture of the developing brain. Toxic stress involves prolonged activation of response systems, such as when a child experiences neglect, adversity, or violence. According to a study by the Center on the Developing Child, toxic stress can lead to underdeveloped neural connections in the prefrontal cortex and hippocampus.[37]

As a result, it is essential to ensure children are placed in environments of high-quality care. Research has demonstrated that many infant care programs and arrangements in the United States result in a lack of quality care. Children in certain environments may not be talked to or

---

36  "Publications And Resources". 2019. California Childcare Health Program.

37  "What Is Executive Function? How Executive Functioning Skills Affect Early Development". 2019. Center On The Developing Child At Harvard University.

played with enough and may have lackluster relationships with caregivers. Moreover, it is less likely that infant care programs will spend much time performing cognitively beneficial tasks, such as reading books, playing music, or providing learning tools. Overall, the evidence illustrates the importance of both individuals and society creating spaces for young children to develop their minds to the fullest capacity.

## LASTING IMPACT OF ENVIRONMENT ON ADULT BRAIN

Now, you may wonder: do environments during childhood affect how an adult brain functions? Martha Farah, director of the Center for Neuroscience & Society at the University of Pennsylvania, led a study to directly uncover how cognitive stimulation tasks at an early age affect brain development in later years. Participants were tracked starting at age four and researchers recorded visits to their homes to measure cognitive stimulation such as the number of children's books, whether toys had teaching purposes, and whether musical instruments were available. The researchers also scored parental figures on warmth and support levels. [38]

When the researchers conducted brain scans on the participants from age seventeen to nineteen, there was a significant correlation between cortex size and amount of cognitive stimulation at the age of four. The lateral left temporal cortex, associated with semantic processing and language comprehension, was the most strongly affected region as a result of early cognitive stimulation. Those with nurturing or stimulating environments at age four

---

38　"Martha J. Farah, Phd – Center For Neuroscience & Society". 2019. Neuroethics.Upenn.Edu.

scored higher on language comprehension exams. Essentially, Farah's research confirmed that the young years are also a critical period that impacts longitudinal cognitive development into adulthood. [39]

## FUTURE-FORWARD:

### Societal Interventions Through Policy

In recognizing the scientific basis of early brain development, what happens for families that may or may not be well-cushioned enough to take that amount of time off and provide the best environment for their children? With that in mind, it becomes valuable to consider alternatives that provide the same enriching environment for your child.

In 1998, First 5 California was founded as a service that brought critical services to millions of parents, caregivers, and children between ages zero and five. Due to California residents' belief in the importance of childhood development between these early years, voters passed Proposition 10. Proposition 10 adds a 50-cent tax to each pack of cigarettes sold, and the tax goes to First 5 California funds. First 5 California has resources such as positive parenting courses, effective interactions and teaching, and early learning and care resources.

Some of the early interventions of First 5 California promote positive parenting and supportive teacher-child interactions. The CARES Plus program under First 5 provided sixteen thousand early educators with resources such as stipends, training, and coaching for teacher effectiveness and

39  Farah, Martha. 2019. "Mind, Brain And Education In Socioeconomic Context". Center For Cognitive Neuroscience.

development. First 5 also created a media campaign between 2003 and 2012 that illustrated the importance of singing and reading to children, particularly for low-income families. The campaign was known as "Talk. Read. Sing." and around 75 percent of individuals increased the amount of time they connected with their children in these manners. [40]

Perhaps the first step is for other states that do not have similar programs to adopt a model similar to that of First 5 California. For those of us who do not have direct access to additional outside programs, the Centers for Disease and Control and Prevention has a program known as "Learn the Signs. Act Early" to help track your child's developmental milestones from two months to five years. Besides the typical physical milestones we may track, such as walking, it is also great to observe cognitive milestones for your developing child.

In 2012, the National Academy of Sciences published a piece with Harvard University to discuss the agenda for the past decades. The objectives included fostering global understanding and awareness of early childhood development, promoting neuroscience and epigenetic research in health sciences, expanding access to early childhood programs, and systematically assessing effects of childhood development programs. Some of the disparities of quality childcare included poverty, the necessary collaboration of social sectors with health, and the increase in local efforts to create a national early childhood development programs. [41]

---

40  "First 5 California". 2019. First5california.Com.

41  "Lessons Learned In Decadal Planning". 2019. Sites.Nationalacademies.Org.

Another question to consider is the people who seek out these resources. Do those most in need recognize the resources available for their children? If not, how can we better promote the available options to families that need it most? If yes, are the resources available enough to ensure each child has the opportunity to develop in an environment that guarantees enriching and healthy brain development? Do these programs really provide each child with the right amount of care to develop into people with brains comparable to those of children who grow up in ideal environments?

These are all issues to continue considering and researching. While it is clear that since 1998, First 5 California has been doing great work to support child brain development, I believe it is time for professionals within both public health and government to evaluate whether the resources provided result in enough equity for children from different socioeconomic backgrounds and locations.

## The Pediatrician's Role in Fostering Healthy Brain Development

In 2010, the American Academy of Pediatrics (AAP) took it upon itself to create the Early Brain and Child Development initiative. This initiative challenges physicians to integrate information about early brain development into their practice of pediatrics. The overall goal is to continue to build healthier childhood communities to ensure the well-being of all children.

Here, they have focused primarily on three areas of change: Advocacy, Point of care/Practice Transformation, and Community Resources/Family Involvement. There are specific goals and objectives for each area, and the AAP is truly aiming to translate scientific research into practices in clinical settings. With this initiative, the AAP is extremely focused on reducing toxic stress in young children as a preventative point.[42]

This may involve screening and identifying children at a higher risk of toxic stress and providing support for parents and caregivers. The initiatives may also involve collaborating with the community and local services to address any concerns that may aid in decreasing toxic stress, as well as increasing communication with social workers, parents, teachers, and other stakeholders in the children's lives to extend efforts of decreasing childhood toxic stress beyond the clinic doors. [43]

**Actionable Ideas:**
1. Write down the primary settings in which you engage with children. Now think of the environments. How do they compare to the list of stimulating positive environments for neural development? What can be improved on by you directly?
2. Think about any pediatricians you know or have encountered in the last few years. Start a conversation about the amazing impact pediatricians can have on early childhood neurological development. Share the link to the AAP initiative here.

---

42    Cheever, Laura W. 2014. "Transforming The Health Care Workforce Through Partnerships". Academic Medicine 89 (Supplement): S8. doi:10.1097/acm.0000000000000356.

43    "Healthychildren.Org - From The American Academy Of Pediatrics". 2019. Healthychildren.Org.

*"Dr. Diamond showed anatomically, for the first time, what we now call the plasticity of the brain. In doing so, she shattered the old paradigm of understanding the brain as a static and unchangeable entity that simply degenerated as we age,"*

GEORGE BROOKS, A PROFESSOR AT BERKELEY,

STATED. [44]

---

44  Sanders, Robert. 2019. "Marian Diamond, Known For Studies Of Einstein's Brain, Dies At 90". Berkeley News.

# CHAPTER 3

# THE PUBLIC INTERVENTIONS TO PROTECT THE BRAIN

---

*"Public health is all around us: the water we drink, the immunizations we receive and the environment in which we live in."* [45]

—BRITTANI BESTERMAN

In the last year of my undergraduate career, I worked as a student assistant in the Maternal, Child, and Adolescent graduate program at Berkeley's School of Public Health. Every time I came into the office, I was fascinated by the research and advocacy efforts of the staff, faculty, and professors who all have an active mission of increasing the well-being of the

---

45  "Who Will Keep The Public Healthy?: Educating Public Health Professionals For The 21St Century". 2004. Choice Reviews Online 41 (05): 41-2850-41-2850. doi:10.5860/choice.41-2850.

world. While I identified as a biology student, I was always intrigued by the public health perspective.

At the end of high school, I had attended a mission trip to Ghana in order to build compost toilets and help with sanitation measures in the villages near Accra. I was fairly oblivious to the culture but found learning to be a two-way street while I was there. We worked directly with Dream Big Ghana, a nonprofit organization that had an established base in Ghana and was fully integrated into the culture and community. Building the toilets from mortar and struggling in the process to carry the water buckets on our heads, we were able to complete two compost toilets for the village in two weeks.

The value in the experience for me was directly engaging with the culture and living the lifestyle these people lived and widening my understanding of what life could be. What I perceived as healthy living or sustainable living was not necessarily the "correct" method or the only method that made sense within our world. I loved the people I met and felt as if true connections had been made through integrating and exploring the other's perspectives. The weekend before leaving, Ghana had a World Cup series against Germany. We all gathered around one small TV, as the volunteers and the villagers were all invested in this shared experience. Although Ghana lost this particular World Cup game, that night is one that will be ingrained in my memory forever.

Back in Berkeley, I helped with administrative needs for faculty who researched the environmental effects of pesticides in relation to population health. In exploring the intersection between brain health and public health, I was determined to discover more about the history of public health interventions in relation to the brain health movement.

Professor Brenda Eskenazi's interest in the human brain began at age twelve when she started dissecting cow and chicken brains for the sake of observing neuroanatomy. While her curiosity grew throughout her childhood, the next time neuroscience crossed Eskenazi's mind again was in 1969. As she attended the Woodstock festival, she quickly realized most individuals were on hallucinogens. On one particular occasion, she witnessed a man jump off a car headfirst into the concrete, convinced that it was water. She was horrified. "I remember walking back from Woodstock for miles in the rain, and wondering what happened to his brain. How had those chemicals distorted his brain?" [46]

Following her interest in the subject, Eskenazi received her bachelor's degree, master's degree, and a Ph.D. in neuro-psychology at The City University of New York. In 1981, she became a postdoc at the Yale University School of Public Health. Soon after her time at Yale, Eskenazi took a position as a professor in the School of Public Health at Berkeley.

In the 1970s, Eskenazi found herself in the midst of a blossoming new field known as neurobehavioral teratology. At the time, the aim of the field was to study the effects of prenatal environmental and chemical exposure on brain development. As a result of a few detrimental environmental events that occurred from the 1950s to the 1980s, many people wanted to explore the topic of neurotoxicity. Eskenazi frequently mentions two events that have shaped her interest in the field: the 1950s mercury spill in Japan and the lead poisoning phenomenon of the 1970s. [47]

---

46   "Brenda Eskenazi". 2019. University Of California Research.

47   Ibid

## JAPAN'S DANCING CATS

In the year 1956 in Japan, residents of Minamata began to notice the strange behavior of cats. These city cats would convulse in "dancing" motions and die rapidly. As the symptoms started to spread to the local individuals, four patients in Minamata were admitted to the hospital as a result of severe symptoms including high fever, convulsions, psychosis, and loss of consciousness. Doctors were puzzled by the symptoms, as thirteen other patients were admitted into the hospital from the same villages. [48]

Soon after, they discovered that a chemical plant named The Chisso Corporation had been dumping methyl mercury in massive volumes into Minamata Bay and contaminating the fish in the bay. People who ate the contaminated fish became ill and suffered symptoms of mercury poisoning. Around 900 people died and 2,265 directly suffered from severe symptoms. Eventually, this health disaster was coined Minamata disease. Minamata disease occurs when methyl mercury enters the central nervous system, causing speech deficits, constriction of visual fields, cognitive impairments, and behavioral disorders. In the *Sunday Star* newspaper and with media outlets all over the world, this area soon became recognized as "Poisoned People."

## THE LEAD POISONING

Another major phenomenon occurred in 1979 and sparked one of the most rapid transformations. Dating back to the Roman Empire, lead was a popular substance for a variety of products, including face powders, mascaras, pigments in paints, condiments, wine preservation, coins, and many

---

48  "Minamata Disease «Sustainability» Boston University". 2019. Bu.Edu.

other household items. For the Romans in particular, lead allowed for an incredibly inexpensive and reliable plumbing system. The consistent consumption of lead paved the road for lead mining in the 1600s. Due to lead's resistance to corrosion, many technological advances utilized lead and by the twentieth century, the United States became the world's leading producer of lead.

In 1921, three General Motor engineers created tetraethyl lead. By 1924, workers were falling sick on a regular basis to the degree of fatality. By 1925, the surgeon general decided to explore the effects of tetraethyl lead on health. Unfortunately, in 1926, the committee of health decided to allow the continued use of tetraethyl lead mixed with gasoline. By 1958, the surgeon general began loosening the regulations on lead usage. As the surgeon general wrote in an official statement, "During the past 11 years, during which the greatest expansion of tetraethyl lead has occurred, there has been no sign that the average individual in the U.S. has sustained any measurable increase in the concentration of lead in his blood or in the daily output of lead in his urine." [49]

Unfortunately, the loosening of regulations around lead had detrimental effects, and individuals suffered the consequences of misinformation. Around 1973, the adverse effects of lead were becoming evident, and the Environmental Protection Agency (EPA) published a document on the "Position on Health Implications of Airborne Lead." The health of the general public was threatened by the continued use and consumption of lead. By December 1973, the EPA tightened the regulations on lead and decreased lead content in gasoline

---

49   "Lead Poisoning: A Historical Perspective | About EPA | US EPA". 2019. Archive.Epa.Gov.

in order to control the adverse effects on health. [50] As illustrated in this situation, despite the early indications of lead's harmfulness, it took a long time to showcase evidence and translate the results into regulatory measures.

> ## "Lead is a potent neurotoxin, affecting the way our kids learn and behave. There is no safe level of lead for children."
>
> –DR. SEAN PALFREY, MEDICAL DIRECTOR, BOSTON LEAD POISONING PREVENTION CLINIC[51]

Through these two events, Eskenazi was inspired to pursue the field and examine neurological teratology. Eskenazi explored a variety of topics, including the impact of different chemicals on the brain and on child development. In 1998, the National Institutes of Health requested study proposals that related broadly to children's environmental health. Eskenazi proposed to study the Salinas area in California, and two years later, The Center for the Health Assessment of Mothers and Children of Salinas (CHAMACOS) was created.

In 2000, Eskenazi started a study that examined 536 children born in the environment of farmworker families in Salinas Valley. Salinas Valley has not only appeared in John Steinbeck's novels, including *East of Eden* but is also known

---

50  "EPA's Position On The Effect Of Airborne Lead". 2019. Www3. Epa.Gov.

51  "Get The Lead Out | U.S. PIRG". 2019. Uspirg.Org.

as the "Salad Bowl of the World" due to its agricultural environment. Due to the high amount of agricultural pesticides in Salinas, the research focuses primarily on a long-term study tracking how exposure to prenatal pesticides during pregnancy affected childhood development. [52]

Researchers took urine samples and blood samples from women while pregnant and at delivery to detect the presence of pesticides in women's bodies. The researchers also took note of the presence of pesticides in participants' homes. For the longitudinal study, every few years, the children's behavior was tracked through neurobehavioral assessments, and physical samples are taken of urine, blood, saliva, baby teeth, and hair. There are around 150,000 existing biological samples in a facility at Richmond, and these samples are used to investigate the effects of these chemicals on CHAMACOS children.

Most of the mothers in the study had detectable signs of exposure to organophosphate insecticides in their urine samples. Organophosphate insecticides break down into two chemicals that can be found in urine samples directly. Based on the research, these chemicals are able to pass through the placenta to the baby's bloodstream. One of the most well-known studies within the CHAMACOS program indicates that prenatal exposure to pesticides has effects on the fetal developing brain. The children whose mothers had the highest levels of organophosphate exposures were at higher risk for neurodevelopmental issues. [53]

---

52  "A Decade of Children's Environmental Health Research". 2019. Epa.Gov.

53  "CHAMACOS Study | CERCH". 2019. Cerch.Berkeley.Edu.

At each stage, deficits could be seen in these children. At six months, the child had poorer reflexes. By age two, these children had higher risks for developmental disorders such as Asperger syndrome. At age five, these specific children showed signs of hyperactivity and attention deficits. When IQ tests were taken at age seven, the children whose mothers had the highest exposure to organophosphate pesticides had lower scores on IQ tests.[54]

A similar study in New York under the Columbia Center for Children's Environmental Health had comparable findings. Children with the highest exposure to pesticides against cockroaches had lower IQs as well. Both pesticides on the farm environment and pesticides against cockroaches contained similar chemicals. Taking the study to another level, the team in New York took MRI scans of children in the study and compared the highest to lowest prenatal exposure. The children with higher exposure to the pesticides had less volume in their prefrontal cortices. [55]

Both of these studies were published in 2011. What has changed since then in terms of public health initiatives or government regulations on these chemicals? Has anything changed at all? While the Environmental Protection Agency (EPA) has acknowledged the dangers of organophosphates,

---

54  Furlong, Melissa A., Stephanie M. Engel, Dana Boyd Barr, and Mary S. Wolff. 2014. "Prenatal Exposure To Organophosphate Pesticides And Reciprocal Social Behavior In Childhood". Environment International 70: 125-131. doi:10.1016/j.envint.2014.05.011.

55  Gochfeld, Michael, and Joanna Burger. 2011. "Disproportionate Exposures In Environmental Justice And Other Populations: The Importance Of Outliers". American Journal Of Public Health 101 (S1): S53-S63. doi:10.2105/ajph.2011.300121.

these harmful chemicals are still tolerated on crops in the United States. Despite the new restrictions made in 2001 on organophosphate usage, the EPA passed thirty-six organophosphate registrations for use in 2013. Regardless of what the studies suggested in the 2011 research, the EPA's concern on the organophosphates seems to be minimal.

According to studies compiled by the Physicians for Social Responsibility (PSR), several environmental factors have direct adverse health issues on brain development: [56]

**Mercury:**

Mercury is a naturally occurring element. In the form of methylmercury buildup, it can be toxic. Areas where high methylmercury can be found include emissions from coal-powered electric plants and fish, including mackerel, ahi, bigeye tuna, and marlin. Studies have shown that mercury at high levels can impair peripheral vision, result in a lack of coordination, and cause impairment of both speech and hearing. Methylmercury exposure as a fetus in the womb directly can impact neurological development.

Symptoms of potential mercury poisoning can include. but are not limited to, terror, neuromuscular changes, headaches, disturbances in senses, and performance deficits in cognitive functions. Treatment usually consists of first removing the source of mercury. If in liquid form, activated charcoal is often used to bind and inactivate the toxin.

---

56  Rauh, Virginia A., and Amy E. Margolis. 2016. "Research Review: Environmental Exposures, Neurodevelopment, And Child Mental Health - New Paradigms For The Study Of Brain And Behavioral Effects". Journal Of Child Psychology And Psychiatry 57 (7): 775-793. doi:10.1111/jcpp.12537.

Gastric lavage is often used to wash out the stomach and intestinal organs.

**Lead:**

Lead can be found in the paint of houses built before 1978 as well as in contaminated soil. Chronic lead exposure can lead to neurotoxicity and damages the nervous tissue. Newborns and young children are at the greatest risk, and lead exposure is correlated with reduced IQ in children and attention deficit disorders. Some of the symptoms of lead poisoning include headaches, behavioral and concentration issues, loss of appetite, nausea and vomiting, muscle or joint weakness, and more. Lead poisoning is most often treated with a chelator. A chelator is a form of medicine that attaches to the lead so the body naturally is able to rid itself of the lead.

In 2013, the Flint, Michigan lead poisoning situation affected between six thousand and twelve thousand children in Detroit. A study in 2017 indicated high levels of lead in around two thousand water systems across the United States. This alarming number affects more than six million individuals in total.

**Polychlorinated Biphenyls (PCBs):**

PCB is a banned chemical previously found in industrial workplaces, in specific fish and shellfish, and contained soils. Even though PCBs are banned, most individuals have a measurable buildup of PCB in the body. Animal studies have demonstrated the effects of low doses of PCBs on the brain. Even at low doses, PCBs can affect plasticity of animal dendrites. Dendrites are the projections from nerve cells that communicate signals to other neurons in the pathway. As a result, PCB can affect learning and memory processes.

Similar to pesticides, no specific treatment exists currently for PCB exposure.

**Bisphenol A (BPA):**
BPA can be found in canned foods, polycarbonate plastics, and epoxy resins. While BPA is known to potentially affect fertility, recent evidence suggests BPA may actually affect the brain as well. In primate studies, BPA has been shown to interfere with building synapse connections between neurons.

**Pesticides:**
Pesticides are used primarily in agriculture settings and homes and are found in contaminated water sources. Due to children's higher respiratory rate, children are more at risk of inhaling pesticides, which can affect brain development. One particular study has also shown that those with high levels of occupational exposure and in agricultural settings have a higher risk of developing brain tumors. Along with that, other studies indicate the increased risk of Parkinson's in populations that have high exposure to pesticides. Pesticide poisonings are commonly underreported. Several symptoms resulting from high levels of pesticide exposure include irritation of the nose, throat, and skin, as well as rashes and blisters. Other symptoms include nausea, dizziness, and diarrhea. Unfortunately, most pesticide poisonings do not have a direct antidote, so interventions that focus on decontamination are generally used.

**Phthalates:**
Phthalates are found in many plastics, cosmetics, and fragrances. In 2018, a study was published that indicates that

phthalates reduce the number of neurons in animal brains. This deficit was observed mainly in the medial prefrontal cortex, which is the region of the brain responsible for executive functions.

These are the current issues that have been highlighted by the majority of environmental health organizations, all of which were slowly researched and recognized in the last half-century.

**FUTURE-FORWARD:**

This research raises several questions to consider. How much of an influence should and do scientific, evidence-based public health studies have on legislation? Can we be confident that legislators will make the population's health and brain health a priority? It has been shown through the Japanese dancing cats and lead poisoning examples that legislation moves slowly and oftentimes primarily as a result of media coverage. Moreover, there are times when legislation is passed after devastating health effects have already occurred. The results of environmental chemicals on the brain are not outwardly evident in most incidences, but that does not mean that proper research should be neglected until the consequences are dire for a large group of individuals. History should not repeat itself.

During my time at the School of Public Health, there was another prominent research study published. Over the course of my senior year, I documented the faculty and professor news coverage in an Excel sheet for the department's grant fund. From the end of 2018 to the beginning of 2019, one of the major studies continuously covered by major media outlets such as the *New York Post* was that of Professor Kim Harley.

**Recent Research on Pesticides**

Harley's recent publication in the Health and Environmental Research in Make-up Of Salinas Adolescents (HERMOSA) program studied 338 children from birth to adolescence. In this study, the researchers examined diethyl phthalate, a chemical used in fragrances and cosmetics. The study recruited pregnant women in Salinas and measured phthalates concentrations for each individual from 1999 to 2000, as well as paragon and phenol concentrations in urine. With this data, the children were later tracked for timing of different stages in puberty. For mothers that had higher concentrations of diethyl phthalate in their urine samples, their daughters experienced earlier puberty. Earlier puberty is defined as precocious puberty. The relevancy holds in that there are studies that suggest precocious or early puberty leads to psychosocial issues for young girls. [57]

This example highlights how the media captured Harley's research heavily during the first two months between December 2018 to January 2019 and how the buzz slowly died down. While the articles may have influenced a small audience, the chances of any sort of action taken by companies using diethyl phthalates are slim to none. Advocacy on brain health matters.

We are the generation that enjoys the benefits of fast information, yet even when it comes to more important actions

---

[57] Harley, Kim G., Katherine Kogut, Daniel S. Madrigal, Maritza Cardenas, Irene A. Vera, Gonzalo Meza-Alfaro, and Jianwen She et al. 2016. "Reducing Phthalate, Paraben, And Phenol Exposure From Personal Care Products In Adolescent Girls: Findings From The HERMOSA Intervention Study". Environmental Health Perspectives 124 (10): 1600-1607. doi:10.1289/ehp.1510514.

taken to protect our brain health, we often let the opportunities slip past us. If more research comes out about specific environmental toxins that harm the brain, will we take action to create positive change in our environments or will we sit back and hope legislators will make the best decisions for us at all times?

Consider Proposition 65 for California. California's Proposition 65 was first enforced in 1986 as the Safe Drinking Water and Toxic Enforcement Act and required the state to publish a list of chemicals known to cause cancer or reproductive toxicity. There are more than nine hundred chemicals listed there. Businesses selling products with chemicals that are on the official list need to include risk warning labels on the package or the product. A "risk" would entail that the level of exposure would cause more than one extra case of cancer in 100,000 people over a seventy-year lifetime. If you walk into any store, these labels are relatively common and are not required to show how much of the chemical the product contains or how you may be exposed to it. While this type of law is beneficial for consumers to decide what to purchase, what about individuals who are exposed to toxins or pesticides or chemicals in their workplace not by choice? It is pretty evident that the state and federal government are not aiming to fully eradicate every known toxin relating to cancer, let alone every toxin relating to brain health. [58]

Legislation is supposed to respond to what the people pay attention to, yet legislation may not go to the greatest lengths to ensure our health. Make protecting your mind and brain a priority.

---

58  "About Proposition 65 – OEHHA". 2019. Oehha.Ca.Gov.

**Actionable Items:**

1. If you work in environments that contain toxins, look them up, regardless of how small an impact your organization claims these substances have on your health. Make sure to understand the full implications of what it means to be in that environment for your health.
2. If you are pregnant, be extremely cautious of the environments you put yourself in, as they may have neurological implications for your child that have not even been confirmed through research or popularized yet.
3. Look at the substances in your makeup or hygiene products. Check the other products you use on a frequent basis. Do they contain diethyl phthalate? Do they contain any of the adverse substances for neurological well-being?

*As the historian Richard Rhodes expressed, "Arguably the greatest technological triumph of the century has been the public-health system, which is sophisticated preventive and investigative medicine organized around mostly low- and medium-tech equipment; ... Fully half of us are alive today because of the improvements."* [59]

---

59 "Public Health Quotes - 10 Quotes On Public Health Science Quotes - Dictionary Of Science Quotations And Scientist Quotes". 2019. Todayinsci.Com.

# CHAPTER 4

# THE TRANSFORMATIVE POWER OF BEHAVIORAL-BASED RESEARCH ON THE BRAIN

As a child, I despised sports. The single type of exercise I enjoyed was my weekly ice-skating lessons that I had started at a young age. At a certain point in time, my parents realized the level of activity I was engaging in was clearly not enough. Most weekends, my dad would take my sister and me to the elementary school nearby to practice basketball techniques.

Having been just barely five feet tall, my involvement in most other sports through middle school remained low. Through a physical education unit, I found a high interest in hurdling and I followed through with joining the track team in the sport of hurdling. In high school, my interest in track and field switched to a different lane, and I began enjoying the 400-meter race. By the last three years of high school, I became a frequent runner and enjoyed running for my cross-country team. Along with that, I followed through with a few half-marathons and external running events like the Santa Cruz Half-Marathon and the Color Run. Each time I exercised, I was aware of the way I felt physically afterward and of being conscientious about my health decisions.

Toward the end of high school into three years of college, I swung to the other end of the spectrum. Like many health-conscious people and women experience, I became overly obsessed with the idea of the perfect body, the perfect amount of discipline. I had changed my diet to vegetarianism and was extremely cautious of what I ate, skipped meals, and was generally orthorexic. I could not go a single day without running six miles, going to the gym, or both, a form of compulsive over-exercising. There was one specific time my aunt visited from hours away to have dinner at a restaurant, and I remember distinctly tearing up because I could not control what I put in my body. Immediately after eating, I went on a six-mile run. There were countless instances of such behaviors that I associated with "being healthy" at the time. Why and how had I skewed my idea of health to the extremes? What did health mean on a societal level, and more specifically, what did it mean to me on a personal level?

Over the course of my senior year in college, I had to reorganize my thoughts and understanding of what healthy living meant. Over the last four years, I had believed health meant a specific body orientation and a specific mindset of perfection and control. Coming out of that mindset meant finding reasons to focus on my health that were not about restrictions or the way I looked. I was guided by an understanding of the impact of my health behaviors on my brain.

Most of us engage in lifestyle behaviors without even realizing the extent to which these choices are impacting our brain health. Every single person has varying motivations for living a healthy lifestyle, but one of the least-cited reasons is to increase brain health. With that in mind, when I was exploring research on brain health behaviors, it was encouraging to find out a lot of what we already choose to do in our individual lifestyles is brain-enhancing.

## EXERCISE ON THE BRAIN

> "Exercise is the most transformative thing that you can do for your brain today."
>
> —WENDY SUZUKI [60]

As a professor in neuroscience and psychology in the Center for Neural Science at New York University, Wendy A. Suzuki has explored one primary factor in brain health for the last six years: physical activity. After receiving an undergraduate degree in physiology from the University of California, Berkeley, Suzuki then went on to earn a Ph.D. in neuroscience from the University of California, San Diego.

While Suzuki's initial research focused on memory and brain plasticity within the hippocampus, she experienced a life-altering shift after she accidentally found herself as the subject of her own experiment in exercise. The hippocampus is the area most attributed to memory and memory function. While during a river-rafting trip, Suzuki felt upset about not being great at the sport during the trip. Suzuki came back home and was determined to build up her strength. With her type A personality, Suzuki modified her lifestyle and

---

60  "Wendy Suzuki". 2019. Twitter.Com.

engaged in kickboxing, dance, yoga, step classes, and every gym class she could pursue. [61]

One afternoon, as Suzuki sat down to write a proposal for a research grant, she noticed for the first time in her life that her grant writing process was going incredibly well that day. Suzuki noted both her ability to focus and the increase in long-term memory. She hit a rapid realization that there might have been some sort of connection between the state of her mind and her newfound love for exercise.

As she looked more into the literature that was already published, she discovered the growing research on physical activity and its connection to cognitive function. Given her high interest in the matter, Suzuki ultimately chose to shift her entire research career toward understanding the effects of exercise on brain health. In a 2018 TED Talk, she advised the public that, "Exercise is the most transformative thing that you can do for your brain today". [62]

According to Wendy Suzuki's research, physical activity alters the brain in two major regions:

### Hippocampus

The hippocampus is a structure involved in memory function. The hippocampus is most prominent in long-term memory formation as well as declarative memory and spatial memory. Declarative memory, also known as explicit memory, is defined as memories related to facts. Spatial memory involves remembering pathways and routes. For example, a cab driver would utilize the hippocampus to

---

61  Suzuki, Wendy. 2019. "Wendy Suzuki | Speaker | TED". Ted.Com.

62  Ibid

navigate directionally through the city and would also use it to remember his passenger's name.

## Prefrontal Cortex

The prefrontal cortex is part of the frontal lobe of the cerebral cortex. As a key player in executive function, the prefrontal cortex has the primary role of attention, working memory, decision-making, personality expression, and complex cognitive behavior. Neuroanatomy studies have shown that the prefrontal cortex continues to develop until around the mid-twenties and is late in reaching maturity compared to other brain structures.

According to Suzuki and her research, exercise can have a wide range of positive effects, both immediate and long-lasting, on the hippocampus and the prefrontal cortex. Previous studies have found that exercise may produce new brain cells and increase the volume of the hippocampus. As for the prefrontal cortex, exercise is shown to improve attention and focus through increased neurotransmitters such as dopamine. "Even more exciting is the finding that engaging in a program of regular exercise of moderate intensity over six months or a year is associated with an increase in the volume of selected brain regions," states Dr. Scott McGinnis, an instructor in neurology at Harvard Medical School. [63]

---

63 "Quickstats:Percentage* Of Adults† Aged ≥65 Years Meeting 2008 Federal Guidelines For Leisure-Time Aerobic§ And Muscle-Strengthening¶ Activities, By Age And Type Of Activity — United States, 2000–2002 And 2013–2015". 2016. MMWR. Morbidity And Mortality Weekly Report 65 (37): 1019. doi:10.15585/mmwr.mm6537a9.

With Suzuki's continued research, her lab is continuing to progress and define the optimal "prescription" of exercise in three primary scenarios. The first theme is discovering what prescription of exercise benefits learning, memory, attention, mood, and academic performance in school and university settings. Moving forward, the second theme is in exploring the maintenance of cognitive functions in adult populations through exercise. The third and final stage is in determining what physical exercises improve both cognition and mood in neurological conditions such as traumatic brain injury, Alzheimer's disease, and Parkinson's disease. [64]

In relation to the general public, the data released in 2018 from the Centers for Disease Control and Prevention's (CDC) National Center for Health Statistics (NCHS) have reported that around 23 percent of adults between the ages of eighteen and sixty-four are reaching the federal activity recommendations. The federal physical activity guidelines recommend a minimum of 150 minutes of moderate exercise or seventy-five minutes of vigorous exercise each week. Less than a quarter of Americans are meeting the minimum threshold of physical activity—27 percent of men and 19 percent of women reaching these standards. Certain regions, particularly the states in the West Coast and Northeast, met the guidelines at a higher percentage than other regions within the United States. [65]

Within the public realm, the fitness industry is a continuously expanding sector. In 2016, based on the International Health, Racquet & Sportsclub Association (IHRSA) report, there was a $27.6 billion industry revenue in the United States

---

64  ibid

65  "National Health Interview Survey". 2018. Cdc.Gov.

and an \$83.1 billion dollar industry revenue on the global scale. In 2019, there is an estimated \$3.671 revenue in the fitness industry, predicted by Statista.[66] This trend in revenue growth may be linked partially to the effects of social media platforms and social media influencers. Within the last decade, there has been an increase in people known as "fitness influencers" on several platforms, such as Instagram and YouTube. People like Nikki Blackketter and Whitney Simmons who have millions of followers dedicate their time to connecting with the public and sharing their knowledge of fitness. Regardless of a large span in audience, social media influencers do not necessarily have the same level of biological expertise as professional researchers and, as a result, the information within current research is rarely translated across social media.

While fitness and the emphasis on physical health through exercise is an incredible benefit for those who value exercise, there is still a large percentage of people who have not considered exercise a priority in life, according to the CDC surveys. The incentives to exercise have not been enough to encourage the general public to engage in consistent physical activity or, conversely, the barriers in finding opportunities to exercise have been greater than the perceived benefits. In the current health advocacy organizations, exercise is portrayed as an opportunity to mainly improve physical benefits.

If physical health is not enough of a motivation for the population to exercise in a consistent manner, is the promotion of brain health an alternative incentive?

---

66    "Only 23% Of Americans Get Enough Exercise, A New Report Says". 2019. Time.Com.

# "Brain aging is more diet than destiny."

–LISA MOSCONI[67]

Similar to Suzuki's interest in physical exercise on the brain, many researchers have been examining the effects of different foods on cognitive functioning. Though there is a general understanding of what foods are best for our physical bodies, there is not that much public understanding of why or what foods are beneficial for our minds.

Although the brain is only approximately 2 percent of the body weight, measurements show the brain accounts for 20 percent of oxygen usage. Hence, the metabolic activity of the brain is remarkable in its magnitude and consistency. In 2008, researchers used magnetic resonance spectroscopy (MRS) to determine products of metabolism of the brain. Wei Chen, a radiologist from the University of Minnesota Medical School, has research results that show two-thirds of brain activity is involved in helping neurons fire and sending signals, while one-third of brain activity is used in "housekeeping." Housekeeping refers to biological processes that help maintain brain tissue and the physical environments of neurons, such as ionic balance. Therefore, the popularized idea of "brain foods" has arisen out

---

67  Camandola, Simonetta, and Mark P Mattson. 2017. "Brain Metabolism In Health, Aging, And Neurodegeneration". The EMBO Journal 36 (11): 1474-1492. doi:10.15252/embj.201695810.

of scientific facts about the brain but may not necessarily reflect research. [68]

One of the primary figures in today's brain food phenomenon is Lisa Mosconi. As the assistant professor of neuroscience and associate director of the Alzheimer's Prevention Clinic at Weill Cornell Medical College, Mosconi has spent years studying the effects of nutrition on human cognition and performance.

From her early research, she became primarily interested in early detection of Alzheimer's through neuroimaging in the form of positron emission tomography (PET) scans. The PET scan can reveal direct evidence of brain activity by applying a radioactive substance to glucose. While the brain uses glucose for metabolism, photons from the radioactive substance will be emitted and detected by a scanning device to illustrate where activity takes place. However, after years of brain imaging in the hopes of identifying genetic risks for Alzheimer's, Mosconi saw little to no evidence. According to Mosconi, Alzheimer's is determined genetically in around 1 percent of the population and for the majority of individuals, Alzheimer's is a result of environment. Alzheimer's is determined by the behaviors that affect our brain health. [69]

---

68  Du, F., X.-H. Zhu, Y. Zhang, M. Friedman, N. Zhang, K. Ugurbil, and W. Chen. 2008. "Tightly Coupled Brain Activity And Cerebral ATP Metabolic Rate". Proceedings Of The National Academy Of Sciences 105 (17): 6409-6414. doi:10.1073/pnas.0710766105.

69  Berti, V., R.S. Osorio, L. Mosconi, Y. Li, S. De Santi, and M.J. de Leon. 2010. "Early Detection Of Alzheimer'S Disease With PET Imaging". Neurodegenerative Diseases 7 (1-3): 131-135. doi:10.1159/000289222.

Along her journey, Mosconi started to notice that participants whose parents had Alzheimer's would ask her about behavioral questions. "Okay, fine. I know my mom has Alzheimer's. What should I eat? What should we eat?" [70] As a result of the common correlation between physical health and food, many individuals were convinced brain health also correlated with food habits.

### Choline:

One of the examples Mosconi cites for food's impact on brain operations is with choline intake. Choline is a type of B vitamin the brain uses to form neurotransmitters such as acetylcholine. Like several other vitamins and minerals, choline is 90 percent derived from food intake and 10 percent formed in the liver. Choline-heavy foods include fish and eggs.

### DHA Fatty Acids:

Foods with high DHA levels are almonds and extra virgin olive oil. Extra virgin olive oil combines both omega-3 and Vitamin E. According to Mosconi, the omega-3s can stay up to two years in the brain following consumption.

### Omega-3 and Omega-6:

The only substance the brain can burn for energy is glucose. The only kinds of fat that can be utilized by the brain are omega-3, omega-6, and omega-9. The brain incorporates these omega fats into the fat of the brain tissue. Foods that fall into this category include flax seeds, walnuts, soybeans,

---

70    Mosconi, Lisa. 2019. "About Dr. Lisa Mosconi — Lisa Mosconi, Phd". Lisa Mosconi, Phd.

chia seeds, sardines, salmon, and mackerel, in addition to many others.

### Glucose-Rich Foods:

The public often has a negative response to glucose, as it is often correlated with bad sugars. However, the brain utilizes glucose for energy, especially in foods naturally high in glucose. Some of these foods include grapes, turnips, beets, rutabaga, chickpeas, bananas, honey, scallions, and onions. Processed sugary foods are not good fuels for the brain, as they are chemically processed and provide a high with a crash.

Other important food sources Mosconi cites are dark leafy greens, berries, and plenty of water. She recently published a book in 2017 I would highly recommend for more detailed advice. The book is called *Brain Food: The Surprising Science of Eating for Cognitive Power.* In the book, Mosconi focuses on busting pseudoscience advice and provides food plans based on her fifteen years of scientific research. [71]

### FUTURE-FORWARD:

Given the research of these two incredible women, as well as many other scientists not highlighted here, the behavioral choices we make can directly influence our brain health. While a lot of us are more prone to believing our choices only affect our physical health, it is essential to realize how much our brain health is affected by our actions.

---

71 Mosconi, Lisa. n.d. Brain Food. Avery/ Penguin Random House.

### Transmitting Research to the Public

The intersection of physical health, exercise, nutrition, and brain health should not and cannot be ignored. Society needs an increased emphasis on our ability to make choices that improve or maintain our brain health starting at a young age. Along that line, another factor to consider is how we can make research regarding brain health behaviors more directly transmittable to the public. As Mosconi stated, there is a lot of pseudoscience, especially about diet fads.

In this day and age, how should researchers and medical professionals increase the transmission of evidence-based information to the public?

This problem is precisely what I have been emphasizing, with the idea that there is a role for everyone within brain health advocacy. Not only is brain health relevant to every single person with a brain, but its advocacy also requires more people to step up to the plate. I find Suzuki and Mosconi incredible, as they have also focused on publications and advocacy. However, a researcher's purpose should be on finding evidence-based conclusions from their topics of interest. There need to be other people established within media and professionals who engage with the public to emphasize topics of importance directly from brain health research. For those of you inspired, I encourage you to join the movement for brain health.

**Actionable Ideas:**

1. Read into research on brain health and behavior. There are plenty of resources online relating to peer-reviewed journals. Always examine the advice given to you. On Google Scholar, search the words "brain health and behavior."

2. If you are not motivated to exercise or to be thoughtful
   of your diet, think through the positive implications for
   your brain health. I encourage you to look up the CDC
   Physical Activity Guidelines. For the next two weeks,
   focus on meeting your own exercise goals that you set
   for yourself.

Today is the day you can implement a few of the suggestions by these researchers into your daily lifestyle and look
into their research further. Change can be gradual, but we
can all increase that conscious effort to improve the long-
term outcomes and future performance of our brains. Pay
attention to your choices that value your brain.

*As Mosconi stated, "We are facing a brain health crisis."* [72]

---

72  Mosconi, Lisa. 2019. "Exploring The Link Between Menopause And
    Alzheimer's". Medium.

# CHAPTER 5

# THE CURRENT STATUS OF MEDICINE ON BRAIN HEALTH

---

*"The physician's highest calling, his only calling, is to make sick people healthy — to heal, as it is termed."*

–SAMUEL HAHNEMANN [73]

"We're starting off with blood pressure," Dr. Lin would state. "Normal." It was like any other typical visit to my doctor's office. Every year, before cross-country season started, I booked an appointment at my family physician's office, and he signed off on the identical yearly physical assessment.

"Temperature 97.8 Fahrenheit. Normal. Now open your mouth wide, and I'll check the back of your throat. Normal." In this particular appointment, much like every other year,

---

73 Hahnemann, Samuel. 2019. "Samuel Hahnemann Quotes". Brainyquote.

my vitals were taken with my blood pressure, height, and weight. All in all, I was out of the clinic in less than ten minutes.

"All good," my physician concluded, as he signed off on my approval form. Heading out of the appointment, I wondered to myself how anyone would ever recognize something was wrong with their brain health. A lot of individuals do not think about their brain health on a regular basis, but as a result of genetic neurological disorders running on my father's side of the family, I was introduced to the possibility at a young age.

Both my grandmother and my aunt had a hereditary form of spinocerebellar ataxia, a disease that caused the degeneration of the cerebellum, with onset after childbirth in this specific type. The cerebellum is the portion of the brain that controls voluntary movement, and spinocerebellar ataxia causes symptoms including uncoordinated gait, abnormal speech, poor hand-eye coordination, vision issues, and difficulty learning and processing information. While I had never met my grandmother due to her early death, I had the opportunity to meet my aunt when visiting Taiwan. At the time I met her, the progression of her disease was rather extreme, and she was reliant on a wheelchair.

How would I know if I had a major issue with my cognitive health or brain structures? The idea that brain health could be dismissed so frequently, especially in the medical setting, shocked me. Yet, as we often do, I let the thought pass. When was the last time you thought about your brain health enough to visit the neurologist? Unfortunately, in the society we reside in, it has become incredibly standard to disregard brain health.

## HISTORY OF MODERN NEUROLOGY

More than a century ago, Jean-Martin Charcot was deemed "the founder of modern neurology" and has often been referred to as the "Napoleon of the neuroses." Charcot was born in 1825, in an era when neurology had not been recognized as a specialty in the field of medicine. Charcot was known to be gifted in painting, and he often used his visual abilities in pathological anatomy. In Paris, Charcot became a professor in pathological anatomy and was credited to give comprehensive clinical descriptions for neurological diseases. Charcot was the first to classify multiple sclerosis (MS) and deem it a distinct disease. By 1868, Charcot was able to create a detailed description of MS, along with detailed illustrations on the differences in pathology in the brain. With his unique skill combination, Charcot was the first physician to diagnose MS in a living patient. For neurology as a field, Charcot increased the importance of clinical observations with pathological findings postmortem, which was extremely essential to the classifications of neurological diseases. [74]

In the United States around the 1870s, the American Neurological Association was formed as the first national society for neurology. In the wider medical community, there was still resistance, as American physicians focused less on specialties. The younger generation of physicians began turning more to specialized fields, and neurology became more common in the early 1900s. [75]

---

74   Kumar, D. R., F. Aslinia, S. H. Yale, and J. J. Mazza. 2010. "Jean-Martin Charcot: The Father Of Neurology". Clinical Medicine & Research 9 (1): 46-49. doi:10.3121/cmr.2009.883.

75   "Historical Overview | American Neurological Association (ANA)". 2019. Myana.Org.

By 1909, three neurologists were able to publicly fund and establish the Neurological Institute of New York, which was one of the first hospitals to care for patients with neurological conditions in North America. The field of neurology and its corresponding organizations were still limited in its ability to lobby. Even in the university settings, it was challenging to have neurology recognized as its own specialty. With the support of the Rockefeller Foundation's General Education Board, the Harvard Medical School was able to successfully establish a training center for neurology by 1930. With the further discoveries of the mechanisms of the brain, the perceived social benefits of the field of neurology grew substantially.

These scientific understandings of the brain included Ramón y Cajal's research, which involved histological methods that revealed the nervous system is composed of single cells that communicate with each other through synapses. The increased knowledge of neurotransmitters and other biological mechanisms within the brain allowed for clinical research that better framed neurological diseases.

By the 1970s, Raymond Adams was another key figure in identifying stroke as a neurological condition. With his expertise in neurology and neuropathology, Adams also was insistent that mental illness should be viewed as a neurological condition. Adams stated that neurology encompasses "all diseases of the nervous system from the simplest disorder of muscle function to the most elaborate psychological derangement such as impaired memory, alertness and attention." Adams was able to combine pathology and physiological research to highlight neurological diseases on a cellular level. [76]

As it is with diseases, having a better understanding of what pathways were disrupted in the brain or what mechanisms were improperly functioning in certain pathologies allowed for the creation of much better therapeutic and chemical interventions. The integration of knowledge surrounding the brain and clinical treatments led to a shift in clinical practice for neurology.

## WHY THE ANNUAL EXAM MATTERS

In a typical manner, a physician performs a physical exam to evaluate the functioning of a person's body. The physical exam includes an updated health history, vital sign checks, visual examinations, and physical examination through external palpation. Oftentimes, screenings will be requested, such as mammograms, breast exams, Pap smears, pelvic exams, and cholesterol tests for women. For men over a certain age, prostate cancer, testicular exam, and cholesterol tests are often recommended screenings. Both genders are also often screened for colorectal cancer, lung cancer, depression, diabetes, sexually transmitted infections, and vaccination updates. Physical exams are one of the most common visits, especially while growing up with an involvement in sports. Not only are annual exams the most common type of examination, but they are also important as the first early detection of many diseases. I am confident many of you have also had or continue to have yearly physical exams to ensure the status of your health.

---

76  Casper, S. T. 2010. "A Revisionist History Of American Neurology". Brain 133 (2): 638-642. doi:10.1093/brain/awp339.

Do you notice any aspect missing from the examinations? At this point, you may have guessed it. What about brain or cognitive health? Should cognitive health examinations be involved in screening procedures? While it can be very beneficial for individuals to directly go to neurologists, there is an inherent cost concern for many individuals.

Depending on the region, neuropsychological services can start at $200 to $400 per hour for private consultations. Taking MRI neuroimaging exams can cost $700 to $7,000 depending on what your insurance covers. For a primary screening of cognitive health, that number may seem like a high price.

Early detection and screenings, which are one of the primary benefits of annual physical exams, do not usually have a comprehensive screening procedure for neurological or cognitive issues. Neurological issues were not perceived as prevalent until the emerging knowledge of brain wellness in recent decades.

It would be beneficial for people after a certain age to receive a cost-effective cognitive screening as part of their physical exams. If any of the results were seen as unusual, the primary care physician would then be able to refer the patient out to a neurologist or neuropsychologist. The biggest benefit this modification could entail is that people who have neurological or cognitive issues would have a much higher chance of early detection.

## WHY EARLY PREVENTION OR DETECTION MATTERS

*"Preventative medicine isn't part of a physician's everyday routine, which is spent dispensing drugs and performing surgery."*

—DEEPAK CHOPRA [77]

Early cancer detection has been extremely advocated for since 1913. The American Society for the Control of Cancer sent forth the message, "With early recognition and prompt treatment, the patient's life may often be saved." The 1940s saw a triumphant movement with the Pap smear. The Pap smear detects cervical cancer and precancerous cells before actual cancer emerges. With the use of the Pap smear, cervical cancer decreased from being the leading cause of cancer death to mortality rates of around 2.4 deaths per 100,000 per year according to the NIH, resulting in one of the clearest cases for early detection in the realm of cancer. [78]

Following World War II, other technologies began to be developed, such as mammograms for breast cancer detection and rectal examinations for prostate cancer. Other statistical data has shown a 25 percent decrease in cancer mortality, even just between 1990 and 2015, partially due to high-quality colorectal and breast cancer screening programs.[79] On the other hand, there are notably potential negatives, including overdiagnosis and overtreatment for cancer as a result of the high level of detection of more abnormalities. However, the case still stands that early detection of cancer is beneficial,

---

77   "Deepak Chopra Quotes". 2019. Brainyquote.

78   "Early Cancer Diagnosis Saves Lives, Cuts Treatment Costs". 2019. Who.Int.

79   "Cancer Statistical Facts"". 2019. Cancer.Org.

especially in regard to slowing down the progression of later stages of cancer.

How do these technologies relate to brain health? It is clear that many people do not get screened for their brain health, yet one in six people are affected by neurological or cognitive issues. Dr. Seth Gale stated, "A major problem of Alzheimer's diagnosis, and ultimately effective treatment, is that by the time the first clinical symptoms appear, irreversible damage to the brain has already occurred." [80] While there may currently be no cure for Alzheimer's, early detection can lead to adopting brain-healthy behaviors or participating in clinical research for therapies.

While brain scans may be the more standard way for neurologists to form neurological diagnoses, there is currently a consensus of validity in cognitive testing. Cognitive testing involves assessments for thinking, memory, language, judgment, and the ability to learn new tasks. While neurologists and neuropsychologists are typically well-versed in giving these exams, there is a neurology rotation that most medical professionals undergo in medical school. In both of my previous jobs at UCSF and Stanford, people like myself who had just earned a bachelor's degree were eligible to run these cognitive exams and surveys with participants in the research setting after proper training. With that in mind, it may not be extremely difficult for primary care physicians to give or present neurological surveys. The question that needs to be considered next is what barriers may occur in incorporating this testing into clinical care.

_______________

80  Gale, Seth. 2019. "Brain Healthy Behaviors Aid Patients With MCI, Mild Dementia". Medscape.

## FUTURE-FORWARD:

### The Neurologist Shortage

According to a publication in the journal *Neurology*, there is a discrepancy in the supply and demand of the neurology workforce. The analysis was performed for years between 2012 and 2025 in the United States. The simulation model took into account the new neurologists trained per year and also simulated the trend of neurological services required. The estimations resulted in around 16,366 neurologists trained in 2012, predicted to increase to 18,060 by 2025. However, the shortage is predicted to be 11 percent in 2012 and increase to 19 percent in 2025. [81]

More neurologists are needed worldwide. Keep in mind the average primary care physician takes about twenty patients per day, while the average neurologist receives between six to ten patients per day. The average wait time for a patient to visit any neurologist was around thirty days in 2012, which is significantly longer than even cardiology bookings.

Even in high-income countries, the lack of neurologists exists. Countries including Canada, Ireland, the United Kingdom, New Zealand, and the United States all have reported shortages of neurologists. Currently, the number of US medical graduates entering the neurology workforce has not kept up with the increasing demand. Neurology as a discipline in medicine is not competing as well as other specialties such as radiology or dermatology, which may happen to provide better compensation or lifestyle flexibilities.

---

81 "The Doctor Won't See You Now? Study: US Facing A Neurologist Shortage". 2019. Aan.Com.

In 2018, the faculty at the University of Texas Health Science Center at San Antonio made changes to medical education in order to inspire more people to pursue neurology as a specialty. The faculty created a novel neuroanatomy elective that was focused on neurosensory pathways, different than before in the way that it was interactive and hands-on. As Dr. Ralph Sacco, a professor of neurology, stated, "The AAN has made a major investment in developing a pipeline program aimed at stimulating more students to choose a career in neurology."[82] Programs like this one may become a trend for the US medical system to increase the number of neurologists.

In Japan, the Japanese Society of Neurology created a fifteen-minute promotion video on the rewarding work of becoming a neurologist. Moreover, the Japanese Society of Neurology launched a free two-day lecture training that focused on neurology. The program cost $70,000 total, but the Society of Neurology considered it to be a good investment in the future of neurology.[83]

Even in areas like Australia where there is not as much of a neurologist shortage, there are issues that involve shortages of neurologists outside of large cities. The ratios were much lower in certain regions including the Northern Territory. As a result, Australia developed a Regional Neurology Committee, solely focused on addressing how to most effectively distribute neurologists across the country and meet the societal demand.

---

82  "Study Suggests 60% Of U.S. Neurologists Experiencing Burnout". 2019. Aan.Com.

83  "About Us | JAPANESE SOCIETY OF NEUROLOGY". 2019. Neurology-Jp.Org.

As for Norway, in July 2019, new strategies were planned for preventing and coping with the growing burden of brain disease.[84] The aims are as follows:

1. Good lifelong brain health, prevention, and quality of life
2. The provision of user-centered care, as well as support for relatives
3. The organization of holistic care from multidisciplinary teams
4. Ensuring adequate knowledge and quality through research and innovation

As confirmed by Professor Tor Aamodt, "Prevention of brain diseases, the provision of equal treatment, follow-up and rehabilitation, as well as increased research and expertise, is absolutely vital in providing patients with optimal outcomes. This strategy will help to facilitate this for a number of brain diseases, including dementia, multiple sclerosis, Parkinson's and stroke-related conditions." [85] The European Federation of Neurological Societies is currently developing a European Brain Health Plan, aimed at raising public awareness of brain diseases and lobbying governments to improve patient and societal outcomes.

Other solutions at the moment are considering telemedicine for neurologists to help make diagnoses in regions where there are shortages or creating a medical team for neurologists consisting of advanced practitioners who are capable of prescribing medicine and providing collaborative care

---

84  "New Strategies And Approaches Needed To Cope With Growing Burden Of Brain Diseases". 2019. Eurekalert!.

85  "Alzheimer's Patients May Face Looming Shortage Of Neurologists – Medicinenet". 2019. Medicinenet.

systems. Although this suggestion would potentially alleviate the high burnout of physicians in neurology, even advanced practitioners may not have enough neurology background to aid in the basics of what neurologists do on a daily basis. However, an integrated model that involves advanced practitioners and nurse specialists seems to be promising. Projects that are working to implement these care teams led by neurologists are being funded and will be evaluated in the near future.

### Systematically Addressing Brain Health

If primary care physicians may be able to focus on the basic neurological cognitive exams at times, it may or may not lighten the load for neurologists who could focus on the items past screening. This is absolutely not to say that primary care physicians should be taking on this responsibility because they too are clearly addressing many patients per day. However, perhaps we need more of a medical shift to ensure that neurological demands can be met in the next few decades, on top of addressing early detection as an important consideration. The issue of brain health does not just fall on neurologists or neuropsychologists but is instead a complication that society as a whole needs to address.

Perhaps additional solutions lie within policy changes. In 2013, 150 neurologists went to Capitol Hill to address and encourage Congress to protect patient access to neurologists. "We want Congress to act now to help alleviate this shortage at a time when the baby boomers are aging and the number of people with Alzheimer's disease is expected to triple by

2050," Dr. Timothy A. Pedley said.[86] Currently, our Medicare and Medicaid systems highly undervalue neurologist services and do not always fairly reimburse neurologists. A study in the United States indicates that six out of ten neurologists are experiencing burnout and work a median of fifty-five hours per week.

Overarching, the question at hand is how we can advocate for a system that prioritizes the best neurological health for our generation. The current system is lacking in early detection services, the number of neurologists, and societal encouragement or space for having annual brain health checkups. However, the population-based issue that one in six people suffer from neurological disorders according to the United Nations report in 2007. In 2017, neurological diseases were found to be the largest cause of disability worldwide with an analysis of 195 countries.[87] As the issue of brain health continues expanding, the deficits of the medical sector gaps need to be addressed sooner than later.

**Actionable Ideas:**

1. Consider what it takes for you to see a neurologist. Consider at what age you might want to start seeing a neurologist on a regular basis and write that number down. Now consider why you chose that age. Think about all the years before the number you wrote down that you may go without the possibility of diagnosing a neurological disorder early.

---

86  Collins, Thomas R. 2017. "Neurologic Diseases Found To Be The Largest Cause Of Disability Worldwide". Neurology Today 17 (22): 1. doi:10.1097/01.nt.0000527316.80068.88.

87  Ibid

2. Are there any neurological or neuropsychological issues
   that run in your family history? If so, have you tried to
   find out more about these diseases and do you follow the
   ongoing related research?


*As Roger Bannister expressed, "I wanted to be a neurologist. That seemed to be the most difficult, most intriguing, and the most important aspect of medicine, which had links with psychology, behavior, and human affairs."* [88]

---

88  Bannister, Roger. 2019. "Roger Bannister Quotes". Brainyquote.

# PART II

# THE NEUROLOGICAL BURDENS: BRAIN DISEASES AND THE PATHWAY OF CULTURAL ADVOCACY

# CHAPTER 6

# THE DECADE-LONG DEVELOPMENTS FOR TRAUMATIC BRAIN INJURIES

---

*"A brain injury is like a fingerprint, no two are alike. A brain injury is to the doctors like the ocean floor is to oceanography, vast and unknown."*

–KEVIN PEARCE [89]

In October of my senior year at Berkeley, I had been focused on the grind of school work with the sole determination to make the most of my final undergraduate year. By this period

---

89  Pearce, Kevin. 2019. "Kevin Pearce Is An American Snowboarder, Aspiring Sports Commentator And Advocatefor The National Down Syndrome Society And The Prevention Of Traumatic Brain Injuries". Kevinpearce.Com.

of time, I was well-adjusted in college and had already found a method of balancing the books with the extracurriculars and everything in between. One of those autumn nights, I headed over to my partner's apartment for a quick study session. Unbeknownst to me, the course of my semester changed from that point forward.

As I briefly traded off my contact lens for glasses, I walked into the kitchen, and in a split second, I slipped backward. While landing straight on my head and still laying in the puddle of water that tripped me, I cried as the hypochondriac in me questioned if I had perhaps caused some mild brain trauma. My partner quickly searched up the "Do I have a concussion?" quizzes on Google and asked me questions in rapid-fire. "Do you have a headache? Nausea? Blurred vision? Mental fog? Fatigue? Sensitivity to light? Sensitivity to noise?" We assumed I didn't have a concussion, but everything in me felt as if I should have gone to get a checkup regardless.

When the weekend passed and Monday rolled around, the base of my neck was still aching, and it felt like an immense effort to even turn my head in either direction. Without further hesitation, I went to the urgent care at the Berkeley's Student Health Center, told the nurses the situation, and was booked in to see the neurologist on the same day. As my first time seeing a neurologist ever, I was nervous about what to expect. Simultaneously, I was concerned that maybe I didn't even need to see a neurologist and that all my concerns would be perceived as illegitimate and metaphorically "all in my head."

When the neurologist approached me, she was extremely kind and listened to my entire situation, validating that getting a checkup was definitely beneficial in these situations. The doctor assigned me to a radiologist who took three

X-rays. As the images were being processed, the neurologist went over a few cognitive and physical exams with me. To my surprise, a large number of these were the exact exams I administered on a regular basis to the participants in my research at UCSF. Some of these memory tasks included repeating a string of numbers, forward then backward. Others included motor tasks to ensure my motor skills were categorized as normal.

When the X-ray images were processed, the neurologist pointed at the images of my spinal cord. "You have very minor cervical lordosis, but everything should go away by itself." After days of dealing with the neck pain from slipping backward, I was relieved to discover I had no perceivable issues with my spinal cord or brain functioning. Although my accident did not lead to a diagnosable concussion, it is estimated that around 3.8 million concussions and around 1.5 million traumatic brain injuries per year occur per year in the United States. This was Kevin Pearce's journey.

At the age of twenty-one, Pearce was a US Olympic pro snowboarder on top of the world, blasted all across the news for years straight as a result of his sports success. In the 2008 Winter X Games XII in Aspen, Colorado, Kevin was nick-named the "Marathon Man" for receiving medals in three top snowboarding competitions. His friend Dean Blotto Gray said that anything you put in front of Kevin on a snowboard, he could conquer.

Almost exactly a year later, December 31, 2009, Pearce's life deviated drastically from his original plans in snow-boarding. While training for a pro trick known as the half double cork, Pearce struck his head on a half-pipe. Realizing the severity of the injury, Pearce was airlifted to the medical center at the University of Utah. He spent thirty-six days in critical care, without a single memory of it at all, and was diagnosed with a traumatic brain injury (TBI). In order to be closer to family, Pearce was then airlifted to the Craig Hospital in Denver, Colorado, where he spent another three months in critical condition. Day in and day out, Pearce fought for his stability, strength, and his former life back. [90]

## THE LOVE YOUR BRAIN FOUNDATION

With the determination and focus that Pearce had always given in his training, Pearce was able to regain an incredible amount of his normal life back. For months on end, he had to relearn how to walk and speak again, step-by-step. Every normal activity we take for granted, Pearce had to learn again. While Pearce is no longer snowboarding at the moment, he has taken all the steps in order to better himself to where he is today after his injury. By 2014, *The Crash Reel* was created as an inspiring documentary on Kevin's life. In the film, he credited a lot of support to his snowboarding friends and his family who had his back the whole way through the journey of recovery. [91]

> Every 11 seconds someone sustains a traumatic brain injury.

—LOVEYOURBRAIN FOUNDATION[92]


90  Picard, Ken. 2019. "Kevin Pearce, Former Pro Snowboarder And TBI Survivor, Rises Again". Seven Days.

91  "Loveyourbrain". 2019. Loveyourbrain.

92  "TBI: Get The Facts | Concussion | Traumatic Brain Injury | CDC Injury Center" 2019. Cdc.Gov.

Through the past few years, Pearce has become an inspirational survivor, motivational speaker, and one of the biggest advocates for brain injury. His campaign is known as the LoveYourBrainFoundation. The foundation focuses on events that educate youth and the general population about concussions and personal responsibility for TBI prevention. Beyond that, LoveYourBrain also hosts fundraising and donation campaigns for those affected by TBIs. The donations help expand programs that allow individuals affected by TBIs to be involved in a community of support.

## THE POPULATIONS MOST AFFECTED BY TBI

Concussions, by definition, are velocity-based injuries that cause brain shaking, resulting in clinical symptoms. In general, concussions may be caused by a direct blow to the head, face, or neck that causes a jolting force on the head. In general, with a blow that does not result in injury, the brain shakes back and forth around thirty times in a uniform manner. With injurious jolts or hits, the brain shakes more rapidly, especially in the corpus callosum region, which is the connection between the right and left halves of the brain. Concussions typically result in short-term impairment of neurological functions. Through the last several decades or so, TBIs have received a dramatic increase in attention, specifically in the arenas of research, medical, and advocacy work. TBIs are considered a public health issue in the United States. In 2014, there were around 56,800 TBI-related deaths in the United States, while approximately 85,000 suffer long-term disabilities due to TBIs.[93]

According to data from the CDC, falls are the most common cause of TBI and unintentional blunt trauma is the

---

93  Ibid

second most common cause of TBI. The age group most at risk from fall-related TBIs are adults age sixty-five and older, accounting for more than two-thirds of the reported TBIs. Contrasting that age group, children at age fourteen and younger are also at large risk for fall-related TBIs.[94]

As for the unintentional blunt trauma TBIs, sports are a common source of such accidents. For boys between ages ten and nineteen, football and bicycling were two of the most common causes, while for girls in the same age range, basketball, soccer, and cycling were the most common causes. In college football, rule changes were implemented in 2013 to decrease the risk associated with TBIs and neck injuries. Ron Courson, a director of sports medicine at the University of Georgia, suggested changes with head-down contact and better enforcement of helmet-contact penalties.[95] The National Collegiate Athletic Association implemented the objective to eliminate injuries from head-down contact and spearing in collegiate football. In the recent editions of the *NCAA Sports Medicine Handbook*, there is a regulation that states, "Any athlete who is diagnosed with a concussion must not return to play or practice that day and must be cleared by a healthcare professional before returning to play or practice." [96]

Along with these primary areas of fall-related TBIs and unintentional blunt trauma injuries, military personnel are also at high risk of TBIs. Between 2000 and 2014, there were more than 320,000 military personnel who sustained TBIs

---

94 Ibid

95 "A Neurosurgeon's Guide To Sports-Related Head Injury". 2019. Aans.Org.

96 "Traumatic Brain Injury: Hope Through Research | National Institute Of Neurological Disorders And Stroke". 2019. Ninds.Nih.Gov.

from the blast trauma of roadside bombs. The majority of TBIs were classified as mild head injuries. [97] As a result of all the above, the CDC emphasizes the importance of knowing the signs of a concussion, or mild TBI. The important symptoms of a concussion or brain injury include one pupil being larger than the other, drowsiness, a headache that does not go away, slurred speech or decreased coordination, repeated vomiting, or loss of consciousness.

Currently, the components assessed in order to determine the existence of a mild brain injury include:
1. Cognitive—an evaluation of concentration, memory, executive functioning
2. Motor—reaction time and coordination tasks
3. Vestibular—balance, vision/oculomotor functioning tasks
4. Physical—neck pain, sleep disturbance, headaches

Although I had no diagnosed symptoms or issues, the truth is that my fall semester turned out to be the least successful semester I had academically. While I had nothing to attribute it to, there are many studies indicating the long-term effects of mild TBIs, which are much harder to diagnose and categorize. A mild TBI is categorized by the American Congress of Rehabilitation Medicine as:

"a traumatically induced physiological disruption of brain function, as manifested by at least one of the following:
1. Any period of loss of consciousness
2. any loss of memory for events immediately before or after the accident

---

97  "American Congress Of Rehabilitation Medicine - An Overview | Sciencedirect Topics". 2019. Sciencedirect.Com.

3. any alteration in mental state at the time of the accident (e.g., feeling dazed, disoriented, or confused); and
4. focal neurological deficit(s) that may or may not be transient

but where the severity of the injury does not exceed the following:

- loss of consciousness of approximately 30 min or less;
- after 30 min an initial Glasgow Coma Scale (GCS) of 13–15; and
- posttraumatic amnesia (PTA) not greater than 24 hours." [98]

While the definition of a mild TBI is relatively specific, the mild TBIs have been hard to diagnose. A minority of those with mild TBIs may have symptoms that persist across time. Researches have also considered how the accumulation of TBI events may present itself as neuropsychological issues in the future. The aggregation of multiple TBIs has been associated with a greater risk of neuro-related health conditions, such as neurodegenerative diseases. In particular, brain injuries on football players have been linked to chronic traumatic encephalopathy. Chronic traumatic encephalopathy is a progressive neurodegenerative brain disease that includes symptoms such as blurred vision, dementia, headaches, mood changes, and memory loss.[99]

## HISTORY OF TRAUMATIC BRAIN INJURY ADVOCACY

In 1951, Dr. Henry H. Kessler and Dr. Howard Rush were two of the pioneers in advocating for physical medicine and rehabilitative efforts. After World War II, Kessler pushed for

---

98  "Glasgow Coma Scale". 2019. Cdc.Gov.

99  "What Is CTE?". 2019. Concussion Legacy Foundation.

rehabilitative physical medicine for veterans. Kessler founded the Kessler Institute of Rehabilitation which expanded from sixteen beds to forty-eight beds when the state of New Jersey provided a grant to the institute. The grant was used for a prevocational diagnostic unit in order to help patients who had a physical limitation to be matched in job placements. This grant allowed the institution to continue to expand into the 1970s and 1980s. In the same era, Rush started to engage the injured pilots from World War II in programs of neurorehabilitation. The pilots were placed in mainly psychosocial and psychological services, along with community-based rehabilitation.[100]

Starting in the early 1970s, there was a significant movement by Dr. William Bryan Jennet to classify brain injuries. In Glasgow, Jennet collected a longitudinal data bank from patients in Glasgow, the United States, and the Netherlands. He wanted to draw a larger amount of importance to secondary ischemic brain damage. Jennet developed the Glasgow Coma Scale, the first reliable and objective way of recording the levels of consciousness of a person after the initial injury. To this day, it is currently the most commonly used system to score consciousness and determine the severity of the potential acute brain injury. In the 1970s, specialized brain injury rehabilitation centers also became much more frequent.[101]

---

100 "History Of Kessler Institute For Rehabilitation". 2019. Kessler-Rehab.Com.

101 Stocchetti, Nino, Giuseppe Citerio, Andrew Maas, Peter Andrews, and Graham Teasdale. 2008. "Bryan Jennett And The Field Of Traumatic Brain Injury. His Intellectual And Ethical Heritage In Neuro-Intensive Care". Intensive Care Medicine 34 (10): 1774-1778. doi:10.1007/s00134-008-1168-7.

By the 1980s, Marilyn and Martin Spivak held the very first meeting at their home in Massachusetts to discuss forming a national association for individuals who had TBIs. After her own daughter's traumatic brain injury, Marilyn faced many frustrations with the lack of services and directions. Both the public and professional understandings of head injuries were lacking. For those like Deb, Marilyn's daughter, who survived TBIs, there was little to no hope. Deb was one of Marilyn's primary driving forces in creating the National Head Injury Foundation, now known as the Brain Injury Association of America (BIAA).

> "This voiceless group are being denied their very basic rights; neurorehabilitation is not a luxury, but is an essential part of the person with acquired brain injury and their family being able to adapt, regain skills, and the support to return to live meaningful lives in their communities."

—BARBARA O'CONNELL, CEO OF ACQUIRED BRAIN INJURY IRELAND [102]

In the first year of its founding, Martin and Marilyn Spivak became the directors of the organization. By 1980, the NIH had conducted The National Head and Spinal Cord Injury Survey, and the results represented one of the first statistical data sets that compiled information on brain injuries.

---

102 "An Interview With Marilyn Price Spivak | Brainline". 2019. Brainline.

By 1982, National Head Injury Foundation advocacy directly led to Congress appropriating $1.5 million in federal funding to new research and training centers for brain injury. More than three decades later, BIAA continues to make major milestones in advocacy, legislation, and research in order to improve the lives of those who have faced a TBI.[103]

In the 2000s, there has been a notable cost reduction in many of the rehabilitative TBI programs and a large push for evidence-based research for up-and-coming treatments. The large number of TBIs associated with the wars in Iraq and Afghanistan have been a catalyst to expand the efforts in research, assessment, and rehabilitation. Meanwhile, the Defense and Veterans Brain Injury Center has been steadily increasing its sites since 1992 to provide support for veterans who have TBIs. As Marilyn Spivak notes, there have been many advances across care in areas such as triage, trauma services, diagnostic technology, neuropharmacology, and rehabilitation services.

## FUTURE-FORWARD:

### Living with a TBI in the Twenty-First Century

A TBI is often termed as the "invisible injury" in that a lot of the time, strangers encountering people with TBIs may not be able to recognize the disease from an outward perspective. Even patients who may seem to recover fully may be dealing with long-term symptoms.

According to a report from the CDC to Congress in 2008, the current interventions are focused on cognitive

---

103 "Homepage - Acquired Brain Injury Ireland". 2019. Acquired Brain Injury Ireland.

rehabilitation and physical rehabilitation. The Cognitive Rehabilitation Task Force evaluated around 270 studies to conclude that cognitive rehabilitation is most effective in the post-acute period. The other commonly utilized method of rehabilitation involves physical rehabilitation, which has also shown to be effective. Physical rehabilitation focuses on enhancing a variety of forms of mobility and increasing strength and endurance to facilitate independence.[104]

However, one of the major life roadblocks may be the ability of individuals with brain injuries to return to work. In the Colorado TBI registry, 50 percent of individuals hospitalized for TBIs were not able to return to work by one year after the injury. Some of the outcomes of TBIs that prevent the ability to return to work include fatigue, transportation challenges, emotional or neuropsychological functioning issues, and even memory issues. Given the widespread scale of this issue, research has suggested that vocational rehabilitation services should also be provided in early rehabilitation stages.[105] Specifically, there are benefits seen in on-the-job training interventions. It has been suggested now that federal or state funding for vocational rehabilitation should increase. For researchers, it has still been challenging to characterize what allows certain individuals with a TBI to return to the workplace successfully and others unsuccessfully.

---

104 Kumar, K Suresh, Selvaraj Samuelkamaleshkumar, Anand Viswanathan, and Ashish S Macaden. 2019. "Cognitive Rehabilitation For Adults With Traumatic Brain Injury To Improve Occupational Outcomes."

105 "TBI Research Review: Return To Work After Traumatic Brain Injury | Brainline". 2019. Brainline.

In order to evaluate the success of TBI rehabilitation, there also needs to be an increased focus on outcome measurements to identify specifically which interventions truly work. Most rehabilitative programs are unique, so validity, reliability, and sensitivity are difficult measures to track within the current system. Currently, the CDC has suggested that comprehensive outcome measures are necessary to identify the tools that are evidently beneficial to TBI patients.

**Research for TBI in the Twenty-First Century**

The other prevalent discussion is on increasing research surrounding TBIs. In cases in which TBI may not be extremely evident, there can sometimes be even a lack of diagnosis. Left untreated, a TBI can have a large effect on someone's mental and emotional capacity. Currently, the most common diagnosis neuroimaging methods used include CT scans and, less often, MRI scans. There has been ongoing promising research regarding statistical machines learning to identify TBIs, which may be another way of diagnosing milder TBIs in the near future.

Beyond better diagnostic methods, there is ongoing research by the Kessler Foundation and other similar labs that hope to determine if virtual reality (VR) therapy can be utilized in the rehabilitation process. There were several publications in 2018 that indicated the potential benefits of VR for TBIs. Special Tree is a rehabilitative resource for individuals with brain and spinal cord injuries. IN 2019, Special Tree incorporated the use of VR technology into their rehabilitation. According to therapist Courtney Fankhauser, "When patients are aware that this is an option, they will be more receptive to using it for their therapy and will realize how essential it is to motivating their recovery." [106]

The National Institute of Neurological Disorders and Stroke also emphasizes the importance of clinical-based research for TBI. Clinical research often requires that individuals with TBI enroll and volunteer in studies to support research on better treatment. Clinical trials for TBI can be found under "TBI and NINDS" under <u>clinicaltrials.gov</u>. Many of the trials will take place across several medical centers across the United States.

Unique clinical observational brain injury research occurs in the realm of biotechnology. In 2018, a team of neurosurgeons and engineers under Prevent Biometrics paired up to create an advanced mouthguard that can detect concussions. The mouthguard is currently known as the Prevent Impact Monitor Mouthguard and detects potential concussions in real-time by measuring distance, angle, and force of a blow.[107] The data is then transferred to a mobile app for further review through the capabilities of Bluetooth.

As of 2019, Stanford's new research project recruited more than one hundred football players in private schools in San Jose to be part of the observational study. Each player has a custom-fit mouthguard with gyroscopic sensors and accelerometers in the front that document how the head is moving. Along with that, videos of the games and practices have been recorded to show the cause of the forces. The aim

---

106 "How Virtual Reality Is Helping Special Tree Treat TBI | Special Tree". 2019. Specialtree.Com.

107 Nelson, Calley, and PhD Samuel Mackenzie. 2019. "High-Tech Mouth Guards Raise Awareness Of Concussion Prevention". Everydayhealth.Com.

is to determine what impacts are causing the most risk of TBIs and concussions as well as which positions are most vulnerable to these types of injuries.[108]

More research needs to be conducted on both the methods of diagnosing and the other potential methods of intervention. The movement and research for TBIs is still in its early phases. It should be one of the priorities to continue the conversation of TBI advocacy into the millennial generation.

**Actionable Ideas:**

1. If you are a parent who has a child in sports, or if you are a person who is highly involved in sports, find a neurologist in the local area who you can contact in any cases of head injuries. Regardless of how small the injury seems, it is important to get checked up. Early intervention plays a large role in the success of your recovery from concussions or mild TBIs.

2. Share the unique research stories on social media. If our generation is to care about our brains, we must start by disseminating relevant information. If you found the research on bioengineering mouthguards for football players interesting, share the link here: https://bioengineering.stanford.edu/news/could-high-tech-mouthguards-help-prevent-concussions. There is always interesting ongoing research in the TBI movement, so find ways to get others informed.

---

108 "Stanford Researchers Study Head Hits In High School Athletes". 2019. Mercurynews.Com.

*According to Pearce, trying to heal his brain has been one of the greatest adversities he has faced. "My best piece of advice would be to rest, relax, and to not get back to your work too quickly. Do not get back to your sport until you're healed. It's so hard to know how long you need to take off, but you go and talk to somebody to find out. The hardest thing to do is to take that action to go and really get checked out by a doctor. As an athlete, the last thing you want to do is to have someone tell you that you can't participate in your sport. I wish that I had taken the right steps." [109]*

---

109 Pearce, Kevin. 2019. "Kevin Pearce - TED Talk". Youtube.Com.

# CHAPTER 7

# THE PROGRESS FOR BRAIN CANCER

—

*"I think it was the first time in his life that science disappointed him. You commit your life and work to science, and then, it's almost like religion: How could you fail me now?"*

—PAUL FISHER [110]

From January to May of 2019, I spent months job hunting. Not one, not two, but five whole months. Being a metric-oriented individual, I kept track of my applications, interviews, acceptances, and rejections on an Excel spreadsheet. I spent a lot of time analyzing those numbers in percentages after landing a job, attempting to understand where I went wrong through the processes and how to improve in the future. I landed my first acceptance at a neurology clinic as a medical scribe in April, yet the location and the cost of living were

---

110 Greicius, Julie. 2019. "'And Yet, You Try'". Stanford Medicine.

unideal for my circumstances. I had to rationalize dropping that opportunity in order to seek more suitable positions but without guarantees of obtaining any other acceptances.

Again, I am thoroughly sharing my experiences beyond the brain health topics concretely addressed so that those of you in similar positions either learn from my errors or are encouraged in whatever relevant capacity. I weighed the pros and cons thoroughly when making the decision to drop the ball on that acceptance. It meant an unknown number of months of anxiety, yet I had twelve more interviews in the queue for positions I felt I could grow in more. I trusted my rationale, and I placed just a mustard seed of faith in my ability to demonstrate who I was and what I stood for at these upcoming interviews. Prior to this, I had applied to more than 155 places in total and had interviews at around twenty-eight locations, with many not resulting in the type of position I was looking for. By the end of my job search, I had interviewed at forty-eight places, resulting in four job acceptances, and one perfect match.

My intention is demonstrating to those coming straight out of college that the process of landing your first job will be extremely challenging. It will be hard to back up your qualifications and to prove yourself to be a candidate worth investing in. That being said, there will be employers out there who see your potential. Do not ever disregard your capabilities due to your age. If you have worked hard, justify where you are and, equally so, where you hope to go in life.

In the few months right after graduation, I started working under the Stanford Center for Clinical Research, which is housed under the Stanford School of Medicine. The research project I currently work on is called the Baseline Project

Health Study, an initiative run by Verily, which is known to be Google's health sub-company. When I began the interview process for the position, I did what I always do for preparation, which involved gathering background information on the mission of the project and the people behind the initiative. In the process, I found the principal investigator's personal experiences and his reasoning for being interested in the collaboration between Stanford and Verily. Here is a portion of the Gambhirs' story in relation to brain health.

Without a doubt, Milan Gambhir was one of the brightest children in the Bay Area of California. Even as a high school student, he researched alongside his father, Dr. Sam Gambhir, at the Canary Center for Early Cancer Detection. Milan loved research, and his questions were endless, especially within the field of cancer. Growing up, Milan had been surrounded with cases of cancer, with his mother having breast cancer and his grandfather having passed away from esophageal cancer.

During the summer, Milan worked under Adam de la Zerda, his bright mind coming up with the potential use of antibodies to detect circulating tumor cells. One specific day during the summer internship, Milan was extremely hard to wake up in the morning, and his mother noted that behavior as odd but dismissed it.

When the Gambhirs rushed to the hospital, Sam asked his pediatric radiology colleagues to be present. The first diagnostic exam was a CT scan, which showed bleeding in Milan's brain. In order to determine the cause of the bleeding, an MRI was taken. It was 3:00 a.m. when the diagnosis came. Milan had a glioblastoma brain tumor.[111]

---

111 Greicius, Julie. 2019. "And Yet, You Try". Stanford Medicine.

## SYMPTOMS OF BRAIN TUMORS

According to the Dana-Farber Cancer Institute, brain tumors are typically found through imaging studies. The signs and symptoms can vary widely based on benign or malignancy as well as the location of tumors.

Some of the symptoms will be nonspecific, which means that some of the symptoms are not just associated with brain tumors. These symptoms include headaches, nausea, or confusion. Other neurological deficits may include loss of coordination, limb paralysis, or sensory changes.

As with many other types of cancer, brain tumors are graded on a scale of one to four, with four being the fastest growing. In most cases, brain tumors are diagnosed with CT or MRI scans. Lumbar punctures, a procedure used to collect a small sample of the fluid surrounding the brain and spinal cord, can be used to screen for cancerous cells. In certain cases, brain biopsies are useful to help with diagnostic testing to check for malignancy. Unfortunately, most brain tumors are not diagnosed until after the major symptoms occur, which can often be a delayed discovery.

## PREVALENCE AND RISK FOR BRAIN TUMORS

For adults, the most common form of tumors are primary brain tumors that emerge in brain cells. These types of tumors are named after the type of cell that becomes cancerous. For example, glial cells that become tumors are gliomas. Meningeal tumors are the second most common type of adult brain tumor. Meninges are the thin layers of tissue covering the brain and spinal cord.

Survival rates are about 34 percent for men and 36 percent for women, with survival defined as living more than five years after initial diagnosis. Again, survival rates vary based on the types of brain tumors. Brain tumors are currently the tenth leading cause of death for men and women in the United States, with around twenty-four thousand adults diagnosed with tumors in the brain or spinal cord. Risk factors for adults include long-term smoking, exposure to pesticides and fertilizer, and working with elements that are carcinogenic. Certain carcinogenic materials include lead, plastic, and petroleum. Although risk factors increase the chances of developing a tumor, risk factors are not the sole cause.

There will be approximately 5,270 brain and CNS tumors diagnosed in children younger than twenty in the United States. Currently, researchers have been examining possible causes of childhood CNS tumors, ranging from genetic to potentially viral reasons. Interestingly, after Leukemia, CNS tumors are the second most common cancer for children younger than fifteen. As with many other tumors, primary brain tumors often begin when cells have errors in the DNA that affect division rates.

Certain genetically inherited syndromes, such as neurofibromatosis and Li-Fraumeni syndrome, increase the risk of brain and spinal cord tumors. Li-Fraumeni syndrome alters a tumor suppressor gene known as TP53. In a normal individual, the TP53 gene creates a protein that keeps cell division under control by stopping cell division of damaged DNA. In individuals with Li-Fraumeni, the TP53 gene is altered so their damaged DNA continues to divide.[112] Changes in the DNA of these cells will increase the risk of developing brain tumors.

---

112  Reference, Genetics. 2019. "Li-Fraumeni Syndrome". Genetics Home Reference.

## THE HISTORICAL ROLE OF BRAIN TUMOR ADVOCACY

In 1973, Susan Kramer and Linda Goldstein came together to discuss the founding of the American Brain Tumor Association. Both of them were facing the loss of their young daughters due to brain cancer. The American Brain Tumor Association was founded in order to support parents and children undergoing treatment for brain tumors.

Currently, the national organization funds brain tumor research and provides information and resources. In 2019, the organization utilized new technology to create a free online support program for nurses, social workers, and volunteers. Beyond that, the organization holds annual national conferences that bring patients, caregivers, researchers, and medical professionals together for an educational program. The educational conference includes information about the latest brain tumor research and treatment.

Another prominent nonprofit organization is the National Brain Tumor Society, founded in 2008. The National Brain Tumor Society aims to affect change across drug development, policy, and research at all levels. There have been more than $38 million dollars raised for brain tumor research grants and awards to researchers across the United States who aim to find treatments for brain tumors.[113]

The National Brain Tumor Society funded the discovery of how glioblastomas depend on cholesterol and how there is a potential treatment by lowering the cholesterol supplies of the tumor. Along with that, NBTS's associated research dollars discover the epidermal growth factor receptor (EGFR) mutations, the most common mutations

---

113 "American Brain Tumor Association". 2019. American Brain Tumor Association.

associated with glioblastomas. The National Brain Tumor Society recognizes the strong presence advocates need to have on Capitol Hill. As a result, Head to the Hill was created in 2012. Head to the Hill is a major opportunity for grassroots volunteer brain tumor advocates to enable those who have brain tumors to have a voice within our government. May is Brain Tumor Awareness Month in the United States. Annually, the Head on the Hill event is held on the first Sunday through Tuesday in May. On that Sunday, the National Brain Tumor Society hosts the Race for Hope DC fundraiser. From Monday to Tuesday, advocates prepare to train and meet with congressional offices to discuss policy issues that matter to brain tumor patients, their families, brain researchers, and doctors. As of 2019, there were more than three hundred advocates representing thirty-four states.

"It is our plan to unite and mobilize the brain tumor community in new, creative ways that can change policies and innovate current standards of care, resources, and knowledge while ensuring that no one is alone when facing a brain tumor diagnosis," CEO of NBTS David Arons said.[114]

## CONVENTIONAL AND UPCOMING TREATMENTS FOR BRAIN TUMORS

Besides the standard treatments for brain tumors, there has been an increasing amount of research in this area. Conventional treatment methods for brain tumors include surgery, radiation therapy, and chemotherapy. Surgery is the most

---

114 "Ways To Give - National Brain Tumor Society". 2019. National Brain Tumor Society.

common form of treatment for brain tumors. A hole is made in the skull, known as a craniotomy, and the surgeon will attempt to remove the entire tumor without damaging vital brain portions. In the case that a tumor is unable to be fully removed, a biopsy is performed to decide how to proceed with further treatment.

In the last few decades, direct delivery chemotherapy and immunotherapy have both been methods developed to specifically target brain tumors. Immunotherapy is utilized to increase the body's natural immune defenses and fight the tumor. Since 2005, immunotherapy has shown promising results in the treatment of brain cancer. As of 2019, the Food and Drug Administration has approved two separate drugs for brain and nervous system cancers that utilize immunotherapy methods. Both types of pills, Avastin and Unituxin, are targeted antibodies that increase the checkpoint inhibitors to prevent cells from becoming cancerous.

At Johns Hopkins University, researchers have been studying chemotherapy localized directly to the brain, known as direct delivery chemotherapy. The researchers at John Hopkins found that in mouse models, the immune system was better maintained for those with direct and localized chemotherapy to the brain compared to those with systemic chemotherapy. Drugs can be injected directly into the cerebrospinal fluid, a liquid that bathes the brain and spinal cord. A thin tube called a ventricular access catheter may be inserted through the skull and into the ventricle of the brain where the drug is then released.

Both immunotherapy and direct delivery chemotherapy have shown a lot of potential for the future treatment of brain tumors. In 2018, data from the Central Brain Tumor Registry of the United States indicated that the relative survival rate was only 34.9 percent for all diagnosed primary malignant brain or CNS tumors. The relative survival rate is measured at survival for five years past diagnosis or start of treatment for the disease. All in all, the relative survival rates for cancer have been increasing since the 1970s. From 1975 to 1977, the survival rates for all cancers was listed to be 49 percent, while the 2008 to 2014 data illustrates that all cancer survival rates are now around 69 percent. However, there is a significant distinction between the all-cancer survival rates compared to the survival rates for those diagnosed with brain cancer.[115]

Interestingly enough, in 2014, there was a paper published on using VR to perform brain tumor resections. This novel tool is known as NeuroTouch, a simulator developed for neurological skill training. It is the most immersive simulator, advertised as a way for residents and neurosurgeons to enhance skills within an immersive VR environment risk-free. NeuroTouch has recently been updated to NeuroVR. NeuroVR is useful in neurosurgical oncology of tumor resections in order to minimize potential damage to surrounding tissues and functional brain areas. The VR has high-resolution haptics, which allows tactile and visual detection of realistic normal tissue versus tumor tissue. Along with that, the VR inputs information about critical anatomical structures and tissue biomechanics.[116]

---

115 "Central Brain Tumor Registry Of The United States - NORD (National Organization For Rare Disorders)". 2019. NORD (National Organization For Rare Disorders).

116 "Neurovr Neurosurgical Simulator | CAE Healthcare". 2019. Caehealthcare.Com.

As of 2012, NeuroVR prototypes were set up in seven teaching hospitals across Canada for beta testing. Researchers will determine later on if VR may become a common part of the training curriculum.[117]

**FUTURE-FORWARD:**

### Early Prevention Methods

For the theme of most chapters in this book, early detection matters. The history of early detection and screening for breast cancer and prostate cancer has been widely beneficial for survival rates. The survival rate for breast cancer was noted to be 91 percent from 2008 to 2014 by the American Cancer Society. In the same realm, prostate cancer survival rates were 97 percent, compared to 68 percent from 1975 to 1977. While some of these high survival rates can be attributed to treatment improvements, yearly screenings for breast and prostate cancer have been invaluable in expanding opportunities for early detection.

With the increasing frequency of imaging for brain issues in general, there has been an increased finding of incidental brain tumors. The concern following diagnosis involves understanding how or if a brain tumor should be treated, in order to increase the best chances of survival for the individual.

In Milan's case, he was a fighter. The brain tumor was 2.5 inches and turned out to be a glioblastoma multiforme, one of the most aggressive forms of tumors originating from glial brain cells.

---

117  Ibid

When Sam Gambhir discovered his son's diagnosis, he contacted an assistant professor in radiology in order to utilize precision medicine for Milan's treatment. Dr. Parag Mallick had researched in precision medicine for decades and was an assistant professor at Stanford as well. Precision medicine focuses on profiling the tumor's DNA, RNA, and protein for molecular analysis to determine whether there are any abnormalities and how the tumor is predicted to respond to different therapies. There is often an issue with the DNA repair, allowing mutated cells to proliferate.

Milan underwent radiation therapy for seven more weeks, and with the strength in his mentality, he was able to successfully complete his sophomore year of high school. Though he was constantly going through chemotherapy, cancer vaccines, and other forms of treatment, he was named a finalist in more than five different science competitions. By summer, Milan had returned to de la Zerda's lab to continue his project on diagnostic devices.

Unfortunately, by November of 2014, Milan came out of remission with a new diagnosis of a tumor at the base of his skull. Through the radiation treatments and the experimental stem cell transplants, Milan demonstrated what it meant to be strong amid adversity. Milan's friends wrote him notes of encouragement on a white electric guitar they purchased for him as a gift. Milan passed away on May 2, 2015. [118]

Sam Gambhir is currently working on early detection of cancers through blood, urine, stool, and saliva biomarkers, with the hope that these biomarkers can be telltale signs of early stages of cancer. Since May 2019, I started working on

---

118  Ibid

this specific project as a research coordinator. The project involves thousands of patients in three different locations, including Stanford and Duke. I am more motivated knowing the purpose behind this work. As I continue to be part of this study, I have high hopes in all the ongoing research on brain tumors.

### The Necessity of Brain Tumor Advocates

As I continue to state within this book, the work surrounding brain health advocacy is not the role of physicians or the sole responsibility of patients with brain diseases. Brain health is about every single person—including you, including me.

From a patient perspective, brain tumors can lead to many neurological problems. Many of the patients who have brain tumors will lose normal capabilities in day-to-day activities such as working or driving. There is a loss of independence of self and a lot of necessary rehabilitation.

Currently, the National Brain Tumor Society is trying to address the issues in health care and advocating for all Affordable Care Act plans to cover treatments at NCI-designated cancer centers. For brain tumor patients in particular and as a result of the rarity, patients would benefit from having coverage for NCI-designated cancer centers. Other policy changes that NBTS supports include the Cancer Treatment Parity Act, which would ensure equal insurance coverage for all cancer treatments regardless of the treatment administration method.[119]

------

119  Ibid

Remember you have the power to support organizations like the ABTA and the NBTS Society and the opportunity to continue to inform yourself on brain tumor research. There are many methods to increase your involvement in brain health, whether you want to join the advocacy through participating in events or hope to demonstrate support through dollars or just want to involve yourself through gathering more education on the topic. Even if it may not directly relate to your current situation in life, brain health matters.

**Actionable Ideas:**

1. Sign up to be an advocate at the NBTS's website. There are a series of free educational webinars that suggest how to be an advocate for brain cancer. There is also a little action-alert tool, which allows you to send an email to the members of Congress regarding topics in public policy that directly or indirectly affect brain tumor advocacy.
2. If you are interested in either of the associations, the ABTS hosts many events and needs volunteers to run the events. There is also an annual Breakthrough for Brain Tumors 5K (BT5K) Run & Walk fundraiser event for those who like running, and proceeds go to the non-profit organization.
3. Recognize Brain Tumor Awareness Month, which occurs in May.

*In 2018, Sam Gambhir received the Benedict Cassen Prize for his research in molecular imaging in his pursuit to expand molecular assays to study diseases including cancer. Gambhir said, "We are in the infancy of a great revolution coming in*

*early disease detection. I am optimistic that the foundations
we have laid in merging the field of cell/molecular biology with
the field of biomedical imaging will lead to significant impacts
in health care for decades to come."* [120]

---

120 "Sanjiv Sam Gambhir, MD, Phd, Receives 2018 Benedict Cassen Prize
For Research In Molecular Imaging – SNMMI". 2019. Snmmi.Org.

# CHAPTER 8

# THE NUMBER ONE LEADING CAUSE OF PREVENTABLE DEATH: THE STROKE

---

*"I essentially became an infant in a woman's body."*

—DR. JILL BOLTE TAYLOR[121]

While I was a teenager, my mother signed me up for weekly acupuncture appointments under the falsified advertising that I would grow taller. To anyone looking for that type of solution, I can assure you I did not grow any taller.

In my clinic sessions, I would always bump into another patient receiving acupuncture therapy for a recent stroke who my parents became friendly with as well. It was incredibly difficult for me to imagine waking up one day to suddenly

---

121 Taylor, Jill. 2019. "My Stroke Of Insight". Ted.Com.

discover you are no longer capable of performing any basic motor skills. For most of us, I believe we imagine we will always wake up with a sound mind and have no difficulties in walking, talking, reading, writing, or recalling any memories. That was the case for Dr. Jill Bolte Taylor.

Taylor had spent years of her life researching mental illness and the biological differences in normal brains compared to the brains of individuals diagnosed with schizophrenia. As a Harvard-trained neuroanatomist, she built her career to become a prominent figure in neurobiology research and an advocate for the National Alliance on Mental Illness (NAMI).

In an incident of irony, Taylor woke up to a pounding pain behind her left eye. The pain gripped and released her over and over again, but she kept on with her normal routine, predicting the feelings would be temporary. As Taylor jumped on her cardio machine, her sense of perception shifted, and she began seeing her own body as peculiar. Navigating to the shower took great effort, and Taylor realized her movements had slowed down massively. When she looked down at her arms, Taylor could no longer define the boundaries of her body, and her consciousness drifted in and out. The moment her right arm became paralyzed, she became incredibly aware there was something wrong with her. Taylor had just self-diagnosed her stroke. [122]

## THE HISTORY OF UNDERSTANDING STROKES

Much to the surprise of most people, strokes were discovered in the 1600s by a Swiss physician named Johann Jakob Wepfer. After studying just four cases, Wepfer was able to diagnose the root cause of stroke symptoms. While observing

---

122 Ibid

a forty-five-year-old patient who suddenly lost all motion and sensation, Wepfer had no diagnosis. Unfortunately, the patient died, and Wepfer still had no understanding of the strange symptoms the patient endured.

In order to better understand the issue the patient had faced, Wepfer began opening the patient's head to locate the potentially problematic areas. As he sliced into the patient's dura mater, the protective outer layer of the brain, he noticed the amount of pooling around the brain. The whole brain, and the areas surrounding the brain, was contaminated by large flows of blood. Interestingly enough, there were no contusions or physical external blows that could have resulted in the patient's symptoms. Wepfer had made the very first diagnosis of the stroke.[123]

A stroke occurs when blood supply to the brain is suddenly interrupted, usually when a blood vessel bursts in the brain, which results in the spilling of blood into surrounding brain cells. As a result, brain cells that normally depend on the oxygen and nutrients from blood die.

In the 1940s, strokes were regarded as a hopeless situation with no potential for treatment. Stroke patients were often combined in observation units, and there were simultaneously no developed prevention or treatment methods. During this decade, the recommendation for stroke patients was to not engage in physical activity. In the 1950s, Thomas Twitchell began studying patient recovery on a larger scale of 121 patients. Twitchell noted that if there were hand

---

123 Pearce, J M. 1997. "Johann Jakob Wepfer (1620-95) And Cerebral Haemorrhage". Journal Of Neurology, Neurosurgery & Psychiatry 62 (4): 387-387. doi:10.1136/jnnp.62.4.387.

movements at four weeks, there was a higher potential for good recovery. [124]

As the newly developed tools for brain imaging emerged with CT scans and MRI scans, imaging the arteries became useful for strokes. Egas Moniz was the first researcher to introduce 3-D imaging of cerebral arteries. The procedure is known as cerebral angiography and allows visualization of the Circle of Willis, the primary artery structure in the brain. Moreover, the more recent categorization of the different types of strokes allows for more specific treatment methods. There are two primary types of strokes, for which treatment is approached in different ways: ischemic strokes and hemorrhagic strokes. Both types of stroke involve similar symptoms, including sudden numbness or weakness, sudden confusion or trouble speaking, sudden trouble seeing in one or both eyes, sudden difficulty walking or with balance and coordination, or sudden severe headache with no known cause.

### Ischemic Strokes

Ischemia is the term used to describe the loss of oxygen and nutrients without adequate blood flow. Ischemic strokes involve a blockage of a blood vessel in the brain, while hemorrhagic strokes involve bleeding in or around the brain. In order for physicians to restore blood flow to the brain, treatment usually begins with clot-reducing drugs known as thrombolytics. The most common thrombolytic used for decreasing brain artery clots are tissue plasminogen

---

124 Raghavan, Preeti. 2015. "Upper Limb Motor Impairment After Stroke". Physical Medicine And Rehabilitation Clinics Of North America 26 (4): 599-610. doi:10.1016/j.pmr.2015.06.008.

activators (tPAs). The tPA method was developed in 2004, so the research on the results is ongoing, although the clinical trials have shown much success. tPA is injected in the arm and can be given up to around 4.5 hours after the symptoms begin. Surgical treatments include carotid endarterectomy, which involves the surgeon making an incision across the front of the neck into the artery, removing plaques blocking the artery.[125]

**Hemorrhagic Strokes**

Hemorrhagic strokes occur when blood vessels in the brain break, causing blood to accumulate in the tissue around the rupture. Hemorrhagic strokes are usually treated with surgical clipping, coiling, or surgical removal as the last resort. For hemorrhagic strokes, it is common for drugs to be given to lower blood pressure in the brain. Surgical methods are also utilized in order to repair blood vessels or stop blood flow at the aneurysm.

Following strokes, rehabilitation therapy is the most common treatment method. Unfortunately, strokes are the primary cause of adult disability, including loss of movement, balance, coordination, and speaking. Speech therapy and occupational therapy are both generally beneficial for patients in the case of loss in language centers. When a patient's condition becomes stable, the focus turns to rehabilitation and prevention programs to avoid another stroke. Currently, there is a focus on motor relearning through constraint-induced movement therapy (CIMT). CIMT is a form of rehabilitation therapy most commonly used for paralysis

125 "How Tissue Plasminogen Activator (Tpa) Works For Stroke". 2019. Verywell Health.

of upper extremities. The therapy involves repetitive movements for several hours a day. Neuroimaging results have shown that the CIMT method can positively shape motor relearning.

While most individuals recognize the aftereffects of a stroke with paralysis, there are also less visible but potential disabilities, including cognitive deficits, emotional deficits, and pain. After a stroke, some individuals may have difficulty with awareness, attention, learning, and memory. Along with that, strokes may occur in brain areas that control emotional processes, leading to emotional difficulties. One of the common disabilities resulting from stroke is depression, which can be treated with antidepressants.

## SUSCEPTIBILITY TO STROKES

As of 2019, strokes are currently the fifth-leading cause of death in the United States. Every forty seconds in the United States, a stroke occurs. Every four minutes, someone dies from a stroke. Around 795,000 individuals suffer strokes each year in the United States, with around 140,000 resulting in deaths. Risks for stroke may include genetics, age, and family history. Older individuals have a higher risk of stroke than the general population. According to the National Institute of Neurological Disorders and Stroke, the risk of stroke doubles with each decade after the age of fifty-five. Men also have a higher risk of stroke—up to 1.25 times that of women. However, statistically, women die of stroke more frequently than men do. [126]

126 "National Institute Of Neurological Disorders And Stroke | National Institute Of Neurological Disorders And Stroke". 2019. Ninds.Nih.Gov.

Contrary to beliefs about brain health, stroke risk is a factor people do have some control over. Research in the Framingham study and Oxfordshire Community Stroke Project proved useful in determining which factors are key players in increasing stroke risk. While some characteristics are unmodifiable characteristics, there are modifiable health factors related to stroke susceptibility. Hypertension, heart disease, blood cholesterol, and diabetes are major predictors of stroke susceptibility. These are important for health professionals to emphasize when discussing strokes, as these are health factors that are more tied to lifestyle decisions. These factors also reemphasize the idea mentioned in previous chapters that physical health is one primary step to maintaining brain health.

High blood pressure increases the risk of stroke by four to six times compared to the risk for those without hypertension. A blood pressure with systolic pressure of 120 mm Hg over 80 mm Hg is considered normal. Values of 140 mm Hg of systolic pressure over 90 mm Hg is considered high pressure. Hypertension tends to increase with age and be more common for men than for women. In extreme cases of hypertension, antihypertensive medication can decrease blood pressure and reduce a person's risk of stroke. As always, consult a licensed medical professional for the best advice given your personal case.

Heart disease is another powerful predictor of stroke. The most common heart disease condition relating to stroke is atrial fibrillation. Atrial fibrillation is an irregular beating of the upper left chamber of the heart, known as the left atrium. Atrial fibrillation causes the irregular flow of blood and can form blood clots that occur in the brain, causing a stroke. Atrial fibrillation can also increase the risk of stroke by 4 to 6 percent. Again, the condition is prevalent in the older population.

Blood cholesterol levels also contribute to heart disease. Cholesterol is produced by the liver and turned into hormones and Vitamin D. Foods high in saturated fat can increase cholesterol levels in the body. With cholesterol, a serum test of 200 mg/dl or less is considered a normal level. Serum levels over 240 mg/dl are considered dangerous and risky for both heart disease and stroke. For both heart disease and cholesterol levels, a healthy diet and regular exercise are both methods of decreasing total cholesterol levels.

## THE PHENOMENON OF THE STROKE BELT

For over forty years, the CDC has collected data on stroke prevalence and risk. Certain states in the United States have consistently had much higher rates of stroke. This phenomenon is known as the Stroke Belt, and the states included are Alabama, Arkansas, Georgia, Indiana, Kentucky, Louisiana, Mississippi, North Carolina, South Carolina, and Tennessee. Interestingly, even when people who were raised in the area move away from these states as adults, they still have higher stroke risk.

According to studies from the University of North Carolina, southeastern states have the most stroke risk factors, including high blood pressure, diabetes, and smoking. The stroke risk factors in these eight states mirror the geographic distribution of stroke mortality. The University of North Carolina collected health data from participants ages forty-five and older, between 2003 and 2007. Among all states, the results of risk factors showed the highest prevalence in the southeastern states. The study also suggested considering

how socioeconomic factors may play a role in health outcomes, especially for lifestyle-related risk factors.[127]

## FUTURE-FORWARD:

### Methods of Stroke Prevention

For those diagnosed with hypertension, atrial fibrillation, or high cholesterol, medications that decrease those
results will also aid in stroke prevention. Currently, anti-
thrombotics are commonly used to prevent blood clots in
arteries, including the arteries in the brain. Along with that,
anticoagulants are often used to reduce stroke by lowering
the clotting property of platelets in the blood. Anticoagulants
are blood thinners primarily used to treat atrial fibrillation.
Antihypertensive medications lower blood pressure and also
aid in reducing strokes. On rare occasions, surgery is used
to prevent or treat vascular damage to arteries in the brain.

While there are several preventative therapies for strokes,
many individuals are unaware of underlying issues such as
high cholesterol, high blood pressure, or atrial fibrillation.
Maintaining these proper metrics is important not only for
heart health but also for beneficial brain health. As mentioned earlier, age brings increased risk of high blood pressure, high cholesterol, heart disease, and diabetes. Along with
healthier habits, smoking cessation and reducing alcohol
consumption can also aid in reducing stroke risk. Even with
an outwardly healthy appearance, it is beneficial to get a
physical exam or a blood draw on an annual or biannual
basis.

---

127 "Stroke Death Rates, Total Population 35 And Older | Cdc.Gov". 2019.
    Cdc.Gov.

If issues in your health metrics are spotted, there are methods to return them to a healthy level, both through lifestyle changes or medication. It is definitely understandable that for some, the cost of having yearly exams with a care provider may seem like a burden. However, keep in mind that the average cost for all strokes in a sample size of 97,374 hospitalizations between 2006 and 2008 turned out to be $20,396 to $23,256, according to the Journal of Stroke and Cerebrovascular Diseases.[128]

Although preventative medicine may seem futile or not a common current concern for you, keep in mind that paying attention to important health metrics may be essential to avoiding high-risk and high-cost health issues, such as a stroke. I encourage you to pay attention to your own indicators of health, especially those regarding brain health.

### Rehabilitation for Potential Strokes

In the rehabilitation realm, there have been studies conducted on how to improve the lives of patients. For chronic stroke patients who undergo intensive rehabilitation, if after a few months there is still low progress, not much more recovery is usually expected. In a study in the Journal of Neurology, Neurosurgery, and Psychiatry, stroke patients participated in an intensive three-week program of ninety hours of therapy in 2019. The increased rehabilitation for the 224 patients in the study led to significant clinical improvements in arm and

---

128 "Journal Of Neurology, Neurosurgery, And Psychiatry | JNNP'S Ambition Is To Publish The Most Ground-Breaking And Cutting-Edge Research From Around The World.". 2019. Journal Of Neurology, Neurosurgery, And Psychiatry.

hand capabilities. More research is required to validate the efficacy of high-intensity programs.[129]

Telerehabilitation, the act of delivering rehab services through the Internet, in another up-and-coming treatment. The in-home rehabilitation was a program devised by Dr. Steven Cramer at the University of California, Irvine School of Medicine. The main foreseeable benefits include convenience, more repetition ability in exercises, flexibility and patient control, and the holistic approach. "I'm pretty optimistic, but I confess that some types of therapy are probably harder than others to effectively practice using a telerehab method," Cramer said.[130] There are a lot of factors to consider, especially that there would be no reimbursement approaches for physicians or health providers who participate. Additionally, there is still unclear evidence as to whether the form of telerehab could be as effective in the long-run as regular in-clinic rehabilitation.


**Future Research for Strokes**

Although technology for functional electrical stimulation (FES) has existed since the 1960s now, its application as a stroke therapy has only become more common since 2004. FES applies small pulses to paralyzed muscles to improve

---

129 Wang, Guijing, Zefeng Zhang, Carma Ayala, Diane O. Dunet, Jing Fang, and Mary G. George. 2014. "Costs Of Hospitalization For Stroke Patients Aged 18-64 Years In The United States". Journal Of Stroke And Cerebrovascular Diseases 23 (5): 861-868. doi:10.1016/j. jstrokecerebrovasdis.2013.07.017.

130 "The Future Of Rehab May Be At Home". 2020. Strokeconnection. Strokeassociation.Org.

the communication between the brain and spinal cord in disrupted areas.

As an example, electrodes can be placed on the wrist extensor muscles. If one contracts the wrist extensor muscles, an electric shock will be triggered. The shock is usually mild in intensity, and the benefits include improved movement and enhanced motor control. In a compiled article, twenty research studies of FES for upper extremities were reexamined to determine the overarching results of FES. According to the twenty studies, FES applied within two months of a stroke had a statistically significant benefit on the outcome of activities of daily living. In 2017, the journal concluded that while FES is promising, there needs to be higher quality large-scale controlled trials to determine the specific degree of benefits.

In 2019, another medically oriented technology was created with artificial intelligence (AI). A study from Google's AI team has been attempting to analyze the risk for cardiovascular disease and strokes using BMI, hemoglobin A1C levels, systolic and diastolic blood pressures, and smoking status. According to the researchers, the algorithms have successfully predicted changes of particular patients who have developed a stroke within a five-year period. Currently, the Google AI algorithm is credited to be 70 percent accurate for this prediction.

According to the CDC, strokes are preventable in around 80 percent of cases if early prevention or detection is successful. The earlier the detection of stroke, the better the chances of mitigating the risks. Other machine-learning, risk-based algorithms are currently using MRI and CT scans to determine whether the stroke is ischemic or hemorrhagic so treatment can be quickly administered. Already, in 2018, the FDA approved Viz.AI Contact, an AI application that analyzes CT scans to detect stroke signs. If the system suspects stroke signs in a particular patient, the neurovascular physician can be alerted about findings through smartphones or tablets. As the trend has shown in the last few chapters of the book, once again, technology holds a lot of potential for preventative health and brain health.[131]

**Actionable Ideas:**
1. Keep in mind that, with strokes, though some individuals may claim they have no control over stroke risks, you do have a certain level of agency in decreasing your risks.
2. Make choices that benefit not only your physical health, but also your brain health, by keeping tabs on diabetes symptoms, high cholesterol, high blood pressure, or atrial fibrillation. Take the reins of your future brain health today.

*"I know it can be very uncomfortable for a healthy person to try to communicate with someone who has had a stroke, but I needed my visitors to bring me their positive energy. Since conversation is obviously out of the question, I appreciated when people came in for just a few minutes, took my hands in theirs, and shared softly and slowly how they were doing, what they were thinking, and how they believed in my ability to recover," Taylor wrote in her book, My Stroke of Insight.[132]*

---

131 "FDA Clears Vizai'S App To Detect And Notify Potential Stroke - Verdict Medical Devices". 2019. Verdict Medical Devices.

132 Ibid

# CHAPTER 9

# THE CURRENT STATE OF MENTAL HEALTH AND DEPRESSION OF THE BRAIN

---

*"I wish people could understand that the brain is the most important organ of our body. Just because you can't see mental illness like you could see a broken bone, doesn't mean it's not as detrimental or devastating to a family or an individual."*

—DEMI LOVATO [133]

In today's day and age, we cannot scroll through any social media platform without seeing posts about advocacy for mental illness. In recent years, while scrolling through

---

133  "Huffpost Is Now A Part Of Verizon Media". 2019. Huffpost.Com.

YouTube, many influencers have also come out with their stories about living with mental disorders. I applaud the diminished stigma around mental illnesses, especially around depression and anxiety.

One of my closest friends works in a mental wellness clinic that focuses on a relatively new treatment for depression known as Transcranial Magnetic Stimulation. While speaking with her, we discussed how the topic of mental illness has become an open conversation, and most people today are quick to admit to experiencing mental illness. "It seems that everyone is open about their battles against depression, as part of their personal experiences," I mentioned. She agreed with me, and we openly theorized on the potential next steps of society, past the state of destigmatization. While admittance has its own inherent value, there must be a societal shift or direction in addressing and improving mental illnesses.

In my formative years, I often felt as if any discussions of mental illness were brushed under the rug. My hypothesis is that this experience came from a mix of growing up in an Asian culture used to concealing all extraneous emotions and feeling a need to present perfectly in the church setting. I had two instances in my life when I was placed in immediate and urgent counseling sessions.

The first visit to the counselor occurred in high school, when my father had just passed away during his in-home hospice. He had spent two years in treatment for colon cancer and my mother and the church had spent two years praying and counting on faith. When faith failed, my mother was blamed. In the school setting, I remained quiet, as I always do when I struggle. My internal adversities have always and will always be my own, yet I had to put on the smile I always did and perform. At the time, there was an extremely heavy push from the school counselor for me to talk to her on a weekly basis. I went there a total of two times, and her question was the same: "Are you okay?" My answer was the same: "I'm fine." There were no tears, no external processing—just internally attempting to understand what this reality meant for me.

When I dwell on my scenario, the same thoughts usually appear. I regret that my father was never able to see me walking down the commencement stage during my graduation at Berkeley and that he had never even been able to hear of my acceptance into college. I regret that my father will never be walking me down the aisle or meeting my future partner or my future children. I regret that my mother has spent years alone at this point and that I cannot always be there to support her in the same way my dad would have. In letting you in on my thought processes, I am solely expressing that there are times that life's circumstances are not ideal. There are people who have circumstances way worse than I ever will, and I empathize with their burdens. In the same way, I see that the progress made for mental illness in the last few decades has been monumental, but I cannot shake the feeling that there is more to be done.

In my conversation with my best friend, we discussed the new tools to combat mental illness in the clinic where she currently works. As we know, mental illness is truly debilitating for some people.[134] Ultimately, mental health affects each and every one of us to varying degrees. Dr. Sherwin Nuland, a former surgeon at Yale's School of Medicine, had fallen into the depths of depression, too.

---

134 Kalanithi, Paul. 2020. "Remembering Sherwin Nuland, The Author Of How We Die, Who Died Last Week.". The Paris Review.

It was a Sunday morning in January 1974. Nuland, at around the ripe age of forty-two, was a successful surgeon. Not only did he have plenty of awards, but Nuland also was amazing at his craft. Yet on that Sunday morning, Nuland was sitting in the kitchen inside a mental hospital. At that point in time, he had spent the last few years ruminating on how his life had fallen apart to such a degree that it could only be described as a mess. In the 1960s, Nuland's divorce had taken a huge toll on him. Though he had tried to save the marriage over the years, it was inevitably not salvageable.

When Nuland began to seek therapy, he realized he had major depression to the extent that he was unable to pick himself up out of bed in the mornings. He would end up intentionally scheduling all of his major surgical cases after 1:00 p.m. because he was unable to get himself out of bed before 11:00 a.m. As his patient referrals decreased, Nuland became increasingly depressed, knowing he was unable to perform to his full capacity as a surgeon. With the advice of his own physician, Nuland admitted himself to the acute care psychiatric unit of the university hospital where he worked. His colleagues encouraged him, "Don't worry, chap. Six weeks, you're back in the operating room. Everything's going to be great." [135] However, six weeks turned into a full-time admission into the Institute of Living, one of the largest psychiatric hospitals in Connecticut at the time.

As Nuland said, remembering his major hospitalization, "When I was hospitalized, my brother sometimes took me home for the weekend, and once, he became infuriated with me. He had tried to talk some sense into me and couldn't,

---

135   Nuland, Sherwin. 2001. "How Electroshock Therapy Changed Me".
Presentation, TED Talk, 2001.

so he hit me with all of his might, just punched me in the jaw, he was so frustrated. But depression grips you from the inside, and no amount of reasoning can change it." The doctors prescribed antidepressants, hoping it would cure his symptoms. They gave him Tofranil and Mellaril, but all the antidepressants had no effect on his mental well-being. When medications had no effect on Nuland, the doctors decided that the time had come to prescribe a prefrontal lobotomy, which involved surgically removing a portion of brain tissue. The prefrontal lobotomy had actually been pioneered in the 1940s at the Hartford hospital, where the Institute of Living was located.[136]

Thankfully, a resident physician at the time stepped in and declared the procedure unreasonable. "I really honestly believe that the basic problem here is pure depression, and all of the obsessional thinking comes out of it. And you know, of course, what'll happen if you do a prefrontal lobotomy. Any of the results along the spectrum, from pretty bad to terrible, terrible, terrible is going to happen. If he does the best he can, he will have no further obsessions, probably no depression, but his affect will be dulled, he will never go back to surgery, he will never be the loving father that he was to his two children, his life will be changed." [137] And with that, the idea of a prefrontal lobotomy was vetoed. The resident then declared that the best treatment to give would perhaps be an electroshock therapy of ten rounds. While every other physician mocked the idea, they were willing to give it a shot. After all, what else could Nuland lose?

---

136 "Sherwin B. Nuland, Author Of 'How We Die,' Is Dead At 83". 2019. Nytimes.Com.

137 Ibid

In the first few rounds of electroshock therapy, Nuland experienced no change. "Plugged me into the wires, put me to sleep, gave me the muscle relaxant. Six didn't work. Seven didn't work. Eight didn't work." [138] At around eleven, Nuland started to feel significantly better, and eventually his depressive symptoms diminished. As Nuland recalled in the early 2010s, "I've had two mild episodes since then. When it happens, I can always tell because I feel myself as this totally incompetent human being who stands right next to this perfectly rational sensible man who says, 'Why are you letting this happen?' yet he has no control over it happening. It takes a little bit of time and more than a few trips to Vittorio. But I can say, when I'm not depressed, I'm the least depressed human being on earth.'" [139]

Nuland went on to publish books on the topic of death and dying, a memoir about his life experiences. The message of this story for Nuland is not to say that electroshock therapy is the method to cure depression at all. Instead, the message is first and foremost that depression is common across the board, regardless of life experiences, status, success, or accomplishments. The second message is that depression treatment for each individual person varies in effectiveness, and new technologies are constantly being developed. The intent not necessarily to stand behind electroshock therapy but rather to keep an open mind toward new developments and therapies that have been validated through clinical research. The third purpose of the story is to segue into how societal perspectives on mental illness have changed through the centuries and how we must continue that progress.

---

138  Ibid

139  Ibid

## DEPRESSION AND MENTAL ILLNESS PREVALENCE

Depression is on the rise. According to the National Institute of Mental Health, nearly one in five US adults live with a mental illness. In 2018, this number rounded to around 47.6 million adults aged eighteen or older living with a mental illness. In 2018, around 4.6 percent of US adults experienced serious mental illness. It is estimated based on the National Alliance on Mental Illness that around 16.5 percent of US youth between the ages of six and seventeen experienced a mental health disorder in 2016. [140]

It is important to not only consider incidences but also the statistics of treatment. In 2018, 43.3 percent of the adult population received mental illness treatment, while around 50.6 percent of youth between the ages of six and seventeen received treatment for a mental disorder. According to the NAMI, there is a significant ripple effect of mental illness. People with depression have a 40 percent higher risk of developing cardiovascular and metabolic disease compared to the general population. High school students with significant depression are more than twice as likely to drop out of school. Caregivers of adults with mental or emotional health issues spend on average thirty-two hours per week on unpaid caregiving. The US economy has an approximate $193.2 billion in lost earnings due to serious mental illness.[141]

Why else might mental illness be a topic of concern, you might ask? For individuals between the ages of ten and thirty-four in the United States, suicide is the second leading cause of death. Overall, suicide is the 10th leading cause of

---

140 "NIMH » Home". 2019. Nimh.Nih.Gov.

141 "Mental Health By The Numbers | NAMI: National Alliance On Mental Illness". 2019. Nami.Org.

death in the United States. While there are differences in age groups, the trend shows an increase in depression for adults and adolescents, particularly over the last decade.

Steven Hyman, director of psychiatric research of the Broad Institute, states that there is an increase in the rates at which mental illness is recognized rather than a drastic increase in incidence. Fortunately, the diminished stigma has also allowed people to feel more open about sharing their experiences with mental illness. However, it is perhaps important to understand that simply opening up about mental illness does not actually address the mental illness. At a time when mental illness has finally been destigmatized, it becomes increasingly important to advocate for mental health treatment or mental illness prevention.

## HOW DEPRESSION APPEARS IN NEUROBIOLOGY

Depression arises from the intersection of multiple factors, including the environment, genes that make people vulnerable, and deficits in neural areas that regulate mood. With the recent brain imaging mechanisms, such as PET and fMRI, one can directly identify the areas of the brain regulating mood and memory.

According to neuroimaging research, the prefrontal cortex, anterior cingulate cortex, and insula are regions most involved in people with depression. The insula is a region of the brain involved in emotional stimuli for emotions such as disgust and negative responses. Studies using neuroimaging have shown that insular volume is correlated with depression scores. Along with that, the anterior cingulate cortex has been used in many neuroimaging PET studies. There is a seemingly decreased activity in the anterior cingulate in people with depression.

Other major factors in depression are the chemical imbalances of the neurotransmitters. However, as Harvard Health noted, the model is currently viewed as an oversimplification. Nerve cell communication involves passing down an electrical signal from the cell body to the axon. At the end of the axon terminal, chemical messengers are stored in the form of neurotransmitters. Neurotransmitters are released into the space between two neurons, and the space is known as a synapse. Once the neurotransmitters travel across the synapse, they can communicate with the receptors on the next neuron and send a signal.

This whole network of communication with electrical and chemical signaling occurs to create any neurologically-based action, including senses, learning, movements, moods, and more. The main neurotransmitters involved in mood include:

1. Serotonin—regulates sleep, appetite, inhibits pain. Certain research indicates low serotonin levels for those with depressive symptoms.
2. Norepinephrine—determines motivation and reward, as well as constricting and raising blood pressure.
3. Dopamine—essential for movement and influences motivation and perception of reality.
4. Glutamate—an excitatory transmitter that plays a role in bipolar disorder and schizophrenia.
5. Acetylcholine—a neurotransmitter believed to be involved in memory, learning, and recall processes.

Research has indicated that people with disruptions in chemical signaling between neurons may be at higher risk and subject to specific mental illnesses, depending on which neurotransmitters are imbalanced.

Aside from neurological conditions, early losses and adverse trauma can result in neuropsychological issues. Certain triggers, such as prolonged stress, may increase stress hormones, which include cortisol and adrenocorticotropic hormone. Genetics has also been accredited to some potential risk for depression. The NIH began funding research for projects observing genome-wide association studies for five major mental disorders. These variations in genes may alter the neurobiology and cellular machinery. CACNA1C is a gene variation that has been linked to brain circuitry involved in emotion, thinking, attention, and memory and is currently studied in relation to major mental illnesses.[142]

## HISTORY OF MENTAL ILLNESSES

Through the centuries, the perception and attitudes toward mental illness have been steadily progressing with increased understanding. During the Middle Ages, mental illnesses were perceived to be intertwined with negative spiritual and religious ideas in many cultures. Negative attitudes toward mental illness persisted to the eighteenth century. In the nineteenth century, Dorothea Dix emerged as a major advocate for mental health care reform. Dix is most known as an activist who drastically altered the medical field throughout her lifetime. She spent many years documenting how the mentally ill were cared for. Dix discovered that the system perpetrated abuse toward people with a mental illness, especially in asylums. Dix created movement through lobbying state legislatures and the US Congress, demanding change.

---

142 "Common Genetic Factors Found In 5 Mental Disorders". 2019. National Institutes Of Health (NIH).

Dix persuaded the US government to fund the building of thirty-two state psychiatric hospitals. In the United States, however, there was still strong stigmatization around people with a mental illness.

In 1887, an undercover journalist visited the Blackwell Asylum in New York. Nellie Bly illustrated the conditions of cruel, harsh, and inhumane treatment. According to Bly, patients described experiences with hydrotherapy, mechanical refrains, and other experimental treatments not validated by research. Some of these early experiments stemmed from the ideas of Henry Cotton, a superintendent at the New Jersey Trenton State Hospital in the early 1900s. Cotton believed infected parts the body correlated to mental illnesses, so his treatment ideas focused on removing teeth and parts of organs including stomach, intestines, thyroid glands, appendixes, and gallbladders. These methods were unreliable cures that led to high mortality rates.

In the 1940s, a German neurologist also experimented with insulin shock therapy, which involved injecting excessive insulin in patients to the point of convulsions and comas. According to Mary de Young, "By 1941, according to a U.S. Public Health survey, 72 percent of the country's 305 reporting public and private asylums were using insulin coma therapy, not only for schizophrenia but also for other types of madness." [143] Other forms of shock therapy included Metrazol shock therapy, which produced symptoms similar to those of seizures as well as retrograde amnesia. Retrograde amnesia is memory loss of events prior to that specific point in time—in this case, before the Metrazol shock therapies

---

143 "The History Of Inhumane Mental Health Treatments | Talkspace". 2019. Talkspace.

were performed. Electroconvulsive shock therapy also gained momentum in the 1940s. Although Electroconvulsive shock therapy had its own side effects, including amnesia, patients with depression often showed dramatic improvements with less obvious side effects than with Metrazol shock therapy or insulin shock therapy.

The mid-1940s brought the development of lobotomies, which involve removing portions of the prefrontal cortex. The prefrontal cortex is the region of the brain credited for intricate planning, complex cognitive behavior, personality, decision-making, and social behavior. As predicted, lobotomies often led to damages that were not repairable and alterations of memory and personalities. Up until the 1970s, it is documented that approximately fifty thousand lobotomies were performed in the United States, particularly in asylums. However, from the 1970s forward, medications became a much more common form of treatment than lobotomies. [144]

In terms of policy, President Harry Truman passed the National Mental Health Act in 1946, which allocated government funds for research into the causes and treatments for mental illness. By 1963, Congress passed another act that provided federal support and funding for community mental health centers. Community mental health centers and local treatment of people with mental illness led to decreased institutionalization as large asylums were closed. By 1979, the National Alliance for Mentally Ill was founded with the intention of providing support, education, advocacy, and research services for people with serious psychiatric illnesses. [145]

---

144 Ibid

145 Ibid

## CURRENT THERAPIES FOR DEPRESSION

Currently, drugs are the most common way to treat depressive symptoms. Antidepressants are generally prescribed for between six months and a year for those being treated for depression for the first time. Antidepressants most commonly target issues with neurotransmitters. Particularly, serotonin pathways are most targeted by these drugs.

These antidepressants are in the form of selective serotonin reuptake inhibitors. In the cell, reuptake transporters will quickly remove the neurotransmitters from the synapse and the signals provided by the serotonin will come to a halt. Instead, serotonin reuptake inhibitors will actually inhibit the serotonin from being removed, prolonging the duration that serotonin will be able to send signals to other neurons. When serotonin remains in the synapse for longer periods of time, there is often an improved mood, which counteracts depressive symptoms. However, the major side effects of antidepressants include insomnia, sleepiness, nausea, and weight gain.

Along with drug therapies, the other common method of treating depression is visiting with a therapist and undergoing cognitive-behavioral therapy (CBT). CBT is based on the idea that patients who have depressive symptoms may have distorted views of themselves, their lives, and their future. CBT aims to shift that mindset and help people modify their damaging behavioral patterns. CBT identifies several main cognitive distortions that can be the root of negative emotions toward oneself or one's life. These ideas of cognitive distortions are most commonly credited to Dr. David Burns, a professor at Stanford in psychiatry and behavioral sciences.[146] Some of these distortions include:

1. All or nothing: the unwillingness or inability to see shades of gray and the idea that everything is at an extreme.
2. Overgeneralization: overgeneralizing one instance into an overall pattern. For example, taking one or two experiences and creating a negative perception of oneself or one's environment.
3. Mental filter: focusing on one negative and excluding all positives in a situation.
4. Magnification or minimization: skewing the perspective to exaggerate the importance or meaning of things or minimizing the importance or meaning of things.
5. Should statements: the tendency to make should statements, which can lead to disappointment in oneself or guilt.
6. Personalization: taking everything personally and believing you are to blame without a logical reason.[147]

Another form of therapy is Interpersonal Therapy (IPT). IPT focuses on relationships as the core psychological issues. IPT aims to help improve a person's communication with others. While therapies are all beneficial and may vary for individual progress, it is important to address and consider altering the social landscape of depression and future innovations for depression therapies.

---

146 Burns, David D. 2012. Feeling Good. HarperCollins.

147 Ibid

### Social Change for Approach to Depression

While neurobiology and neuropsychology are often the methods of intervention for depression, perhaps it is important to venture outside these typical forms of treatment to observe depression from a societal standpoint. According to Dr. Michael Bader and a journalist named Johann Hari, it is undeniable that some people do get better with only antidepressants. However, addressing neurobiology and solely using pharmacological approaches becomes a limited, one-dimensional treatment. The potential for more efficacy in depression treatment can come through forms of building social support.

For example, Hari cited that when people with depression feel cared for by researchers, the rates of improvement are at a high 40 percent. Hari discusses many other forms of social disconnections that may factor in depression. While the social stigma has been steadily decreasing over the last few decades, the next issue to address is how to build a social-based therapy that compliments that ongoing treatments for antidepressants or other forms of cognitive therapy.

We should also consider whether we should be equipping our children with the tools to understand emotional regulation and mental illness at a much earlier age. In 2016, the US Preventive Services Task Force recommends general practitioners to include universal depression screenings for any individual over the age of twelve. While the medical world is a place where mental illness can be detected, is there a better place in which adolescents can be provided with tools to understand or navigate mental health? Schools are where most children learn about puberty on a yearly basis. What if mental health was included in that discussion, in a manner that allowed the youth who may be struggling to reach out? What if stress coping techniques or emotion management techniques were introduced to students at a younger age? I recognize that if I had such techniques to address mental illness at a much younger age, I would have benefited a tremendous amount. I vouch the same case for others as well.

As stated in prior chapters, everyone has a role. If you are a social scientist or a person who loves to come up with actionable societal solutions or if you are a social psychologist, you can be involved in brain health. If this work is of any interest to you, perhaps researching or creating social-based movements just so happens to be within your expertise.

### Innovations in Research for Depression

According to recent research at Harvard Health, newer treatment options are being developed under transcranial magnetic stimulation (TMS). TMS is a noninvasive method of stimulating the brain externally. By applying strong magnetic fields to areas of the brain that are involved in mood regulation, one can stimulate the neurons in these areas. TMS does not require anesthesia and is usually well-tolerated. Around 50 to 60 percent of people who do not respond to pharmacological treatments respond well to TMS. The research study cited by Harvard Health indicated that one-third of individuals who undergo TMS will have full remissions, so symptoms of depression have not relapsed. The average time of repeat treatment is around once per year for the treatment time to last.

The procedure is rather quick. The first place the technician or physician targets is usually the motor cortex, a noticeable landmark in the brain. After that, the team will search for the dorsolateral prefrontal cortex, an area shown to improve symptoms of clinical depression when stimulated. Usually, treatment lasts for several weeks for about twenty to fifty minutes per session.

The FDA began allowing marketing of TMS for depression in 2008, and since then, many clinics have come out with TMS-based depression therapies. As per usual, what matters most is that TMS research continues in order to confirm the efficacy of such treatments and that one checks the validity of the clinics marketing TMS to ensure the use of proper protocols and procedures. While Nuland found electroshock therapy to be useful, and while many find TMS to be useful, be proactive in informing yourself before making your decisions, especially with choices regarding your brain health.

**Actionable Ideas:**

1. Jot down three ways we could change the social structure in order to equip our children and the next generation with cognitive tools. Consider the primary areas in which you interact with younger individuals, whether as a teacher, mentor, or friend. What are the tools you have to learn in your life to address mental illness? How could these methods of handling mental illness be taught to our children at a younger age?
2. Look up research centers or clinics in your area that focus on addressing mental illness. Keep an open mind if you are someone who has never sought out help for mental illness before. Go to the homepage of three clinics or research centers around you and just simply read their about page. Be bold enough to seek help if you recognize you are struggling.

*And lastly, as proclaimed by Nuland as a person who has overcome the curveballs and difficult moments thrown at him with strength: "If I, with the bleakness of spirit, with no spirit, that I had in the 1970s and no possibility of recovery, as far as that group of very experienced psychiatrists thought, if I can find my way back from this, believe me, anybody can find their way back from any adversity that exists in their lives."* [148]

<hr>

148 Ibid

# CHAPTER 10

# THE INCREASING PREVALENCE OF ALZHEIMER'S AND DEMENTIA PREVENTION PROGRAMS

———

Loss is transformative, to say the least. There is something about loss that has motivated me in my lifetime. As Malcolm Gladwell eloquently put it, eminent orphans are people who have experienced the loss of at least one parent before their eighteenth birthday. Statistically, this is around one in twenty children according to the US Census Bureau. Loss can propel people to chart their own lives in ways others who have support systems may not need to.

According to Lucille Iremonger's Phaeton Theory of 1970, people who show exceptional personal achievement in certain fields have frequently experienced childhoods marked by parental loss through death. The study in the *Journal of*

*Psychohistory* included eminent US writers and presidents and one hundred Americans who were labeled to be most influential through *Life* magazine. Of these three categories of people, bereavement was common for those included in *Life*. The study indicated that eminent Americans showed substantial levels of parental loss and nearly three-fourths had experienced difficult childhoods due to some sort of loss. Although the study indicated results that supported the Phaeton Theory, there were inconclusive results, as correlation does not always equal causation.[149]

Regardless, for a lot of us who want to make a difference, the negative experiences in our lives can actually be formative in how we envision improving our society for those around us. For Dr. John DenBoer, loss played a significant role in his life missions, especially within the world of neuropsychiatry.

I resonated with DenBoer as he described the emotions he felt in losing his grandmother to Alzheimer's disease (AD). DenBoer's grandmother, Jean Seeling, developed dementia five to ten years prior to her passing, and DenBoer experienced the devastating loss of mentally losing someone extremely dear to him. From that point forward, DenBoer's mission was set: dementia prevention.[150]

---

149  Standing, Lionel. 2020. "Exceptional Achievement And Early Parental Loss: The Phaeton Effect In American Writers, Presidents, And Eminent Individuals". The Journal Of Psychohistory.

150  Psych, Mental. 2019. "Clinical Neuropsychologist Phoenix | Mental Edge Psych". John DenBoer.

<blockquote>
"Hardships often prepare ordinary people for an extraordinary destiny."

—C.S. LEWIS [151]
</blockquote>

## THE NEUROBIOLOGY OF ALZHEIMER'S AND DEMENTIA

As many of us know, AD is a progressive neurodegenerative disorder, and AD makes up approximately 60 to 80 percent of dementia cases. Often, symptoms of Alzheimer's begin with difficulty remembering recent events and names, apathy, and depression. Later progressive symptoms include worsening memory, impaired judgment, confusion, behavioral changes, and difficulty speaking, swallowing, and walking.

Currently, in clinical research, AD is classified into three phases. The first phase is a presymptomatic phase. People who are cognitively normal but have higher amyloid deposition are in the first phase of AD. In the brain, amyloids are formed from soluble proteins that become insoluble fibers that are resistant to degradation. Mutated genes can cause the production of excessive amounts of toxic protein known as amyloid-beta peptides. These peptides will build up and form amyloid plaques. The second phase of classification involves amyloid deposition with evidence of neurodegeneration. Those in the second phase may often experience progressive cognitive decline at higher rates than expected based on age. In the third phase, cognitive impairment can actually interfere with daily activities.

---

151  "Hardships Often Prepare Ordinary People For An Extraordinary Destiny. -C.S. Lewis - Google Search". 2019. Brainyquotes.

Along with high amyloid-beta levels, the neuropathology of AD also involves the buildup of tau neurofibrillary tangles. Within the brain, tau is a brain-specific, microtubule-associated protein. Both tau and amyloid-beta proteins are directly correlated with the negative symptoms of AD. Having accumulation of plaques and tau tangles can damage and destroy the synapses between neurons that allow for memory and cognition. Amyloid-beta usually occurs before tau tangles, and amyloid-beta can convert normal tau to a toxic state. The feedback loop involved allows toxic tau to enhance amyloid-beta toxicity.

Besides Alzheimer's, other neurodegenerative disorders also fall under the category of dementia, such as vascular dementia. Vascular dementia is most commonly caused by strokes in the brain, which can result in damage to the surrounding areas where the blood vessel is damaged. A lot of memory-based functionality occurs in the hippocampus, a structure in the brain primarily credited for retaining memories. Dementia is divided into major neurocognitive disorder for cognitive declines in more than one domain and mild neurocognitive disorder for modest declines that do not interfere with everyday activities.

## THE RISK FACTORS FOR ALZHEIMER'S AND DEMENTIA

There are many risk factors for AD, including age, education level, head trauma, family history, and APOE-e3, or -e4. APOE-e3 or -e4 is a gene correlated with specific risks for AD. Over 60 percent of individuals with AD have one APOE-e3 or -e4 gene. In an independent study through the Global Alzheimer's Association Interactive Network, more than fifty-eight thousand subjects were recruited to examine APOE-e4 effects on AD. Women who carried one or more copies of the e4 allele for a protein known as Apolipoprotein E (APOE) had a greater risk of developing AD. Early-onset of AD can also be attributed to mutated genes for amyloid precursor protein (APP).

However, genetics are not the only factors involved in AD. Environmental factors and behavioral health choices seem to play a role as well. According to the Alzheimer's Association, head injuries can be linked to the risk of dementia. Additionally, there is a head-heart connection that links heart health to brain health, for vascular dementia in particular. Other risk factors for vascular dementia include those discussed in the previous chapter regarding strokes. Of these, cholesterol levels, smoking, diabetes, and high blood pressure are all characteristics relating to stroke and vascular dementia risk.

## THE HISTORY OF ALZHEIMER'S RESEARCH

In 1906, Dr. Alois Alzheimer first diagnosed Auguste Deter with memory loss, paranoia, and psychological changes. Deter was only fifty years old, yet she was placed in a psychiatric hospital as a result of the symptoms of AD. In the autopsy, Alzheimer noted in his report that there was shrinkage in and around her nerve cells within the brain. Alzheimer examined the brain using specific stains that revealed what we now term as amyloid plaques and tau neurofibrillary tangles.

Alzheimer went on to publish many descriptions and case studies of similar patients through 1909 and 1910. By 1931, electron microscopy had been developed and allowed for more detailed images on the autopsies of brain tissue. Through the 1960s, Sir Bernard Evans Tomlinson and Sir Martin Roth, psychiatrists in Britain, began to hypothesize that the plaques may be related to AD.[152]

---

152 "Alzheimer's Disease Fact Sheet". 2019. National Institute On Aging.

By the 1970s, researchers began to deviate from the plaque hypothesis and started to observe the neurotransmitter acetylcholine. Acetylcholine is a common neurotransmitter in the hippocampus, and the theory named a deficit of acetylcholine as a factor in causing AD. By 1974, Congress established the National Institute on Aging (NIA), an organization that supports AD and dementia research. Fortunately, by 1984, amyloid-beta proteins were identified in people with Down syndrome and AD. Because Down syndrome is a disorder that requires a third twenty-first chromosome, researchers began researching the twenty-first chromosome. On the twenty-first chromosome, amyloid-betas were identified as responsible for the plaques in the brain.

By 1993, the FDA approved Cognex as a drug treatment for AD. The drug targets memory loss and dementia symptoms. The FDA also approved specific cholinesterase inhibitors. Cholinesterase inhibitors are one of the most common medications for memory even today that stabilize cognitive symptoms. These drugs inhibit the breakdown of acetylcholine, a neurotransmitter involved in learning and memory. Commonly prescribed cholinesterase inhibitors today include donepezil, rivastigmine, and galantamine.

Several presidents also contributed to the awareness and movement in AD research. In 1994, President Ronald Reagan announced he had been diagnosed with AD, leading to greater awareness of the disease through media coverage. In 2011, President Barack Obama jumped on board with the National Alzheimer's Project Act, which serves as a national funding source for research in these areas.

## SMART BRAIN AGING

A clinical neuropsychologist, DenBoer earned his master's degree at the University of Colorado, followed by a Ph.D. at the University of Montana. During his internship, he held dual academic appointments at both Harvard Medical School and Boston University School of Medicine. Through Mental Edge Sports Psychology, one of his earlier organizations, DenBoer started an active sports psychology practice. With his success in training elite tennis athletes in improving performance, DenBoer has become a consultant for several organizations, including Arizona State University and the United States Tennis Association.

After years of researching dementia, DenBoer decided that, in order to make the greatest impact in the field of dementia, he wanted to create a company that provided dementia mitigation and intervention. Dementia mitigation focuses on targeting mild cognitive impairment (MCI), which is defined as a slight but noticeable and measurable decline in cognitive abilities involving memory and thinking skills. Individuals who develop MCI have a large risk of developing AD or other forms of dementia. Three years ago, in Phoenix Valley, Arizona, DenBoer started SMART Brain Aging.[153]

When I asked DenBoer how his company stood out from his competition, he replied, "We are a research group turned into a company, not a company that does research. SMART Brain Aging is driven by the mission and not the profit." The researchers within the company took more than five years of clinical trials with three thousand participants at Harvard Medical School and Boston University School of Medicine.

---

153  "SMART Brain Aging". 2019. Smartbrainaging.Com.

In quantifying numbers, the programs proved to delay the progression of the disease up to 2.5 years and reduce the negative cognitive impact by 45 percent. The program is covered by Medicare and is available at a multitude of clinics within Arizona.

Besides the in-person clinical program, DenBoer developed Brain U Online, which features more than twenty thousand exercises that target executive functioning, processing speed, speech and language, memory, and attention. It is the first and only scientifically supported digital therapy program developed specifically for aging adults who want to maintain healthy brain function and those suffering from the early stages of dementia.[154]

With the continued goal of validating the science and research behind the interventions presented in the programs, DenBoer has paired up with UCLA to run more clinical trials. Having just started in 2018, the collaboration between UCLA and SMART Brain Aging is projected to grow and expand the clinical trials to ideally more than three hundred people. DenBoer has even taken several opportunities to engage people who can really benefit from early mitigation.

In early April 2019, the documentary *This is Dementia* was released on Netflix as a collaboration between Netflix and DenBoer. Premiered at FilmBar in downtown Phoenix, the documentary followed DenBoer's journey and mission of mitigating the onset of dementia. Overall, DenBoer has utilized every opportunity to work toward his vision, and his hard-earned success has been recognized.[155]

---

154  Ibid

155  Ibid

**FUTURE-FORWARD:**

### Early Intervention Procedures

In our generation, we face the devastating reality that many of us are at risk for cognitive impairments at an older age. Currently, dementia affects more than sixty million people worldwide, and the number is predicted to triple in the upcoming decade. Every three seconds, another individual in the world develops dementia, according to the World Health Organization. While it is essential that we focus on the physical aspects of health, we also need to turn out attention to the often subtle declines of brain health with aging. As shown in DenBoer's study, when mild cognitive impairment occurs, there are methods of engaging the brain that do delay the onset of dementia. In the upcoming years, more programs like DenBoer's will be bound to come out.

Early intervention within neurological diseases like dementia leads to the best possible results. Due to the fact that most dementia and AD diagnoses occur at later stages when the symptoms are already very apparent, it is necessary to consider how society can have earlier intervention methods. In one of the conversations I had with DenBoer, he mentioned the vulnerable group was usually fifty-five years and older.

Hearing that, I suggested that perhaps at fifty-five years, it should become standardized for older adults to have annual or biannual appointments with clinical neuropsychologists who can detect notable changes in cognitive function or confirm the health of our brains. This proposal would be similar to that of mammograms for women, which are yearly performed procedures to check for breast cancer after the age of twenty-five. DenBoer showed great enthusiasm for the proposal and agreed it would be a beneficial method to detect abnormalities in cognitive function early on and address interventions in a more effective time frame. If you are an older individual, perhaps it is time you get to know your clinical neuropsychologist and have your cognitive state checked.

The tools a neuropsychologist may use to diagnose AD or dementia include neuropsychological surveys that assess the degree of impaired memory and cognitive skills. Laboratory tests may be used to rule out other causes for similar symptoms, including potential Vitamin B-12 deficiency or thyroid disorders. For AD in particular, brain imaging scans can also be used as part of the diagnosis to rule out other causes, such as brain tumors or hemorrhages. The most common technology used for AD diagnosis includes MRI and CT. PET scans are currently being developed to detect tau tangles in the brain, and other diagnostic methods are up-and-coming as well.

**Alzheimer's Disease and Quality of Life**

As with many of the neurological diseases discussed, there are plenty of nonprofits working on AD advocacy. The Alzheimer's Association is one of the largest nonprofit funders of AD research. The organization is fully focused at both the federal and state policy levels and recruits Alzheimer's Ambassador volunteers. In 2019, the Alzheimer's Association is currently lobbying to ask Congress to increase AD and dementia research funding at the NIH by $350 million in the 2020 fiscal year. There are plenty of other advocacy groups also pursuing incredible feats.

As with debilitating and degenerative diseases, AD often requires a tremendous amount of care planning for affected individuals, families, and caregivers. The model suggested by the Alzheimer's Association is a person-centered care model. This involves several steps that the organization suggests as recommendations:

1. Know the person living with dementia
2. Recognize and accept the person's reality
3. Identify and support ongoing opportunities for meaningful engagement
4. Build true authentic relationships
5. Create and maintain a supportive community for individuals, family, and staff
6. Evaluate care practices regularly and make appropriate changes

**Actionable Items:**

1. Reflect on your own personal experiences with loss. How have these shaped you?
2. Look up the Alzheimer's Association. Is there an organization in your area? Go to the volunteer page. What type of volunteer opportunities catch your eye?
3. If you know of someone who has dementia or engage with people who have dementia, I would highly recommend you look at the Person-Centered Assessment and Care Planning model in further depth.

*DenBoer's vision is as follows:*
*"A world where societies understand that dementia is not a natural part of aging and individuals can take action to reduce the impact of the disease."* [156]

---

156 Ibid

# PART III

# THE MIND INNOVATORS: WHAT THE FUTURE HOLDS FOR BRAIN HEALTH

# CHAPTER 11

# THE VALUE OF WELLNESS PROGRAMS ON TARGETING BRAIN HEALTH

—

*"If you ask what is the single most important key to longevity, I would have to say it is avoiding worry, stress and tension. If you didn't ask me, I'd still have to say it."*

—GEORGE BURNS[157]

As a full-time intern at a growing company, I had my first glimpse into the concept of corporate wellness. Once every few weeks, the company I worked for would hold a mandatory intern meeting to discuss the workforce culture of wellness. There was an incredible emphasis on ensuring

---

157 "George Burns Quotes". 2019. Brainyquote.

employees were well taken care of both mentally and physically, as well as a support system that encourages employees to make wellness goals for themselves.

In valuing transparency, I admit I am someone who preaches wellness habits but has a difficult time maintaining or pursuing them within my own life. Through college, I had developed extreme ideas of productivity and the hustle culture. I was rounding myself up to about four hours of sleep, from 2:30 a.m. to 6:30 a.m. on a usual basis. I had set this standard in my own mind that I needed to study an average of seventy-two hours per week, on top of working fifteen hours, interning in research for about fifteen hours, and engaging in about twenty hours of additional extracurricular activities. If I had not sat in the library for at least five days and accomplished at least 80 percent of my study hours that week, I deemed myself too slow in my progress. Being in the top quartile of the class was mandatory for me. I had turned myself into a metric-based machine, and my components were always under self-critique. I preached mindfulness, and I convinced myself I was taking care of myself by the act of exercising and eating healthily. But on I neglected the other side of self-care.

After graduating from my undergraduate years, one of my criteria for choosing a role within a company was how comprehensively a company cared for employee health. As a Stanford employee, the university provides a lot of wellness programs. Under the BeWell program, employees are encouraged to participate in a yearly health screening, which involves getting tested for specific blood measurements and speaking with a health coach on upcoming goals. Along with that, the program also has monetary incentives up to $500 for reaching self-created health goals or participating in the free exercise or stress-meditation courses at the gym. Other resources Stanford provides for staff include free ergonomic evaluations and free gym memberships. In the same realm, many other companies are also hopping on the bandwagon to provide high-level health and wellness programs for employees.

Currently, I am learning what self-care means to me. My definition of mindfulness lies in giving myself enough space, time, and kindness to be able to pursue my life visions to the fullest:

I want to be a physician in the future, one who is able to dedicate my full attention and my full capabilities to my patients. I am aiming to establish a nonprofit health organization by my early thirties for those with spinal cord injuries and their caretakers. I hope to work as a site physician for spinal cord research at some point in my life. In terms of the creative aspects of who I am, my entrepreneurial sides are daring me to create a podcast and a popularized medical blog by my late twenties. I want to produce an album and create a recording studio with profits for public health causes by my forties. Through the course of my life, I am definitely going to paint more paintings and publish many more books.

These are my honest life visions, which continue to be refined as I learn more about how to move closer to my aims on a monthly basis. With all this in mind, I have such a specific idea of how I want my life to turn out, and although neglecting my wellness for the first twenty-two years of my life turned out fine, I cannot keep doing that. There is value in investing in my wellness. There is undoubtedly value in investing in your wellness, too.

In the last decade, wellness programs have reached the forefront of the corporate world, marketed specifically to companies for employees. The purpose of employee wellness is to advocate for a better company aggregate health, both emotionally and physically. For employers, one of the primary motivations to engage with these programs is the potential for health care costs to be diminished for employees as a result of healthier lifestyles. Within the United States, this particular sector has grown to an $8 billion industry.[158] Wellness programs typically consist of asking participants to fill out health risk questionnaires, hold medical screenings, and encourage engagement in short courses on both nutrition and exercise.

While Adrian Gore grew up in a home that focused a lot on education, he never imagined the success that he would come to attain in his career. In his high school days, the actuarial route really appealed to Gore and as he graduated college, he entered his first job at Liberty Life. Gore was intoxicated by the scale of impact that an organization could have. Shortly after that, Gore started his first business through Discovery Limited and continued on to the path of entrepreneurship by founding Vitality in 1997.[159]

Vitality is the longest-running wellness program that offers a biometric risk assessment through screenings, personalized health recommendations and goals, and methods paired with incentives to take action toward health goals. It is offered to companies across the globe and allows employers to track both engagement and population health. While Vitality was extremely successful in the realm of wellness

---

158  Fallon, Ivan. 2019. "Interview: Vitality Boss Adrian Gore Is In For The Long Run". Thetimes.Co.Uk.

159  Ibid

programs, Gore jumped on another opportunity to expand the abilities of the program.

## VITALITY

One of the major programs currently recognized and provided by many companies is Vitality. Gore, a South African billionaire, founded Vitality in 2008. As a Forbes CEO, he also owns leading financial services institution in South Africa known as Discovery Limited.

As quoted from the Vitality Institute, "Vitality takes a data-driven approach to changing behavior based on an actuarial science model with proven results in achieving individuals' meaningful and measurable health improvement and works with forward-thinking companies that are committed to improving the health and well-being of their workforce while improving their bottom line." [160]

When the Apple Watch was released in April 2015, Gore was immediately drawn to the opportunities it brought to health and fitness tracking. Without hesitation, Gore began to plot how best to incorporate the Apple Watch into Vitality, which was already reaching millions of insurance customers by this point. In less than a few days, he had a breakthrough idea—to let members fund their Apple Watches through the incentive of physical activity. Gore requested that his team draft up an idea and engagement strategy before reaching out to Apple to pitch the concept.

On May 13, 2015, only one month after the release of the Apple Watch, Gore took a plane halfway around the world. From Johannesburg, he found himself in Cupertino, California, for a one-hour meeting with Apple's Chief Operating

---

160 Ibid

Officer Jeff Williams and Vice President Doug Beck. Gore had compiled a short presentation of his vision in the collaboration between Apple Watch and the millions who utilized Vitality.[161]

> "Have a purpose for your business beyond making money. I have always wanted to make a difference in a positive way, even if I didn't know right from the start what I wanted to do at a granular level."
>
> —ADRIAN GORE [162]

The product structure is unique in that it gives the policyholders the watch for a nominal upfront activation fee and has the users commit to a monthly payment for it. If the person met the physical activity target, their payments would be covered by the insurer. If not, the policyholder paid but did not have to pay more than if they had just purchased the product. Williams and Beck were intrigued by the idea that the watch could be funded by an actuarial surplus it was helping to create. Apple's team stressed that partnerships were not common but that they were interested in exploring further with Vitality. After several more meetings and discussions, in September 2015, Vitality launched the Vitality Active Rewards with Apple Watch in South America, the United Kingdom, and the United States.[163]

---

161 Ibid

162 Ibid

163 Ibid

Currently, the programs are personalized. All the data are measured, allowing for insight and verification of the benefits of activities. The company is driven by data but is still people-oriented. Vitality's data indicates a 12 to 15 percent decrease in insurance claims for engaged members and also a 91 percent client retention rate.[164] The program itself focuses on human-centric health and behavior changes and has a strong interest in the brain wellness sector. In several of their programs, there are stress-reducing techniques and exercises aimed at reducing the negative effects of stress on both emotional well-being and the physical brain.

## DIFFERING PERSPECTIVES OF EMPLOYERS AND EMPLOYEES

In a recent survey by the RAND Corporation, around 69 percent of companies with over fifty people have wellness programs. According to the RAND Corporation, there are three major purposes for wellness programs:
1. Screening to detect health risks
2. Lifestyle management to reduce health risks and encourage healthier lifestyles
3. Disease management to support individuals with chronic conditions[165]

Around 21 percent of the programs evaluated in the survey were intervention-focused, which included the incorporation of lifestyle management and disease management. Another 20 percent of the programs were focused on screening but held limited services for lifestyle or disease management.

---

164 Ibid

165 "RAND Corporation Provides Objective Research Services And Public Policy Analysis". 2019. Rand.Org.

Thirty-four percent of the programs were considered very limited in screening, lifestyle management, and disease management services.[166]

*Forbes* also published a survey in 2018 indicating how employees are influenced by the wellness programs available. The statistics illustrate that 87 percent of employees consider health and wellness packages when making decisions about employment. Sixty-seven percent of employees who work under organizations with wellness programs enjoy their jobs more. Fifty-four percent of Generation Z and 58 percent of millennials surveyed indicated that wellness programs are very important in their job decisions. However, many employers are skeptical about making the initial investment in providing wellness programs.

Zirui Song and Katherine Baicker, researchers from the University of Chicago and Harvard, performed a large-scale, randomized, controlled trial on the efficacy of wellness programs. In 2019, the research findings illustrated that wellness programs did not result in a measurable difference in health measures within the eighteen months that the programs were given.

Baicker stated, "The optimistic interpretation is that there is no way we can get improvements in health or more efficient spending if we don't first have changes in health behavior. But if employers are offering these programs in hopes that health spending and absenteeism will go down, this study should give them pause." [167] As the dean of the Harris School of Public Policy at the University of Chicago, Baicker's view

---

166 Ibid

167 "Workplace Wellness Programs Fail To Improve Health, Study Finds". 2019. University Of Chicago News.

may be the dominant one in health policy. Based on their findings, wellness programs have not yet proven to decrease employee health care costs. While other studies have contradictory results that demonstrate positive improvements as a result of these wellness programs, the consensus is that the adoption of healthy behaviors is proving difficult to implement on a large scale.

## STRESS ON BRAIN HEALTH

From a noneconomic perspective, wellness programs may be beneficial for managing employee stress and increasing employee productivity, both of which were not measured in the study above. In 2007, an American Psychological Association survey indicated around 74 percent of respondents cited work as a primary stressor in life.[168] There have been several notable publications on the effects of stress on hypothalamus and amygdala functioning. The hypothalamus is a portion of the brain that maintains homeostasis through controlling hormone release, regulating body temperature, and managing thirst and hunger. The amygdala is a portion of the brain involved in processing emotions, primarily fear.

Within neural networks, the hypothalamus and the amygdala are both involved in mitigating stress. In stressful or threatening situations, the amygdala is activated and signals to the prefrontal cortex and the hypothalamus. As stated in a previous chapter, the prefrontal cortex is the area responsible for problem-solving and emotion processing and regulation and is basically the control center. In turn, the hypothalamus will send out a hormone called

---

168 "Stress in America: The State of Our Nation. Stress in America Survey." PsycEXTRA Dataset, 2017. https://doi.org/10.1037/e515932017-001.

corticotropin-releasing hormone. The corticotropin-releasing hormone will activate a region of the brain called the anterior pituitary gland. The anterior pituitary gland sends out the adrenocorticotropic hormone. The adrenocorticotropic hormone activates the adrenal glands, which are responsible for producing cortisol. Cortisol is known as the primary stress response hormone.

In normal settings, cortisol is highest in the morning and during exercise. Consistent high cortisol levels can result in prolonged "fight or flight" symptoms. Cortisol may increase blood pressure and heart rate. Other symptoms of high cortisol may be rapid weight gain in the face, chest, and abdomen. Mood swings, osteoporosis, suppressed immune systems, and digestive problems are just a few other potential symptoms.

## HOW STRESS CAN BE MITIGATED BY WELLNESS PROGRAMS

Therefore, it is important to recognize the physiological damages that can come with prolonged stress. In considering the damage prolonged stress may have on overall health, perhaps the movement toward wellness programs is commendable in specific areas. Of the wellness programs explored in different settings, there is evidence that intervention programs can have beneficial effects on stress management.

In order to determine if participation in a wellness-based mindfulness stress reduction intervention decreased psychological distress and medical symptoms, 103 people were recruited to the study at a university in West Virginia. Fifty-nine people were placed in the intervention group and forty-four in the control group. After an eight-week stress-reduction program focused on mindfulness meditation techniques for the intervention group, the subjects reported significant decreases in psychological distress and medical symptoms. The measurements utilized included the Daily Stress Inventory and the Medical Symptom Checklist. According to the follow-up questionnaire, the decrease in both psychological distress and medical symptoms for the intervention group were maintained past the three-month mark. The study indicated that mental and physical health can be influenced by stress reduction interventions in wellness programs.

In 2003, a similar intervention was given to medical students. The formal name of the intervention is known as Mindfulness-based Stress Reduction (MBSR). Second-year students participated in the ten-week seminar on MBSR. The baseline mood was scored at the beginning of the study for both the control and MBSR group. Despite the MBSR group having a greater score for the baseline total mood disturbance (TMD) measurement initially, the MBSR group ended up with a significantly lower TMD score after the study ended. Given the results, this study also concluded mindfulness interventions can be beneficial.

Now, you may be wondering what happens in mindfulness-based wellness programs. How can mindfulness interventions impact the brain?

There are two primary ways individuals can alter stress: from an external or internal perspective. One can modify the stressor by eliminating the external stressor, but that is rarely possible for those who do not have such financial liberty to toss away their job. The other method is altering the internal perspective of the stressor. MBSR has been promoted in both psychological and medical fields and defined as two primary aims:

1. The self-regulation of attention
2. Being open and accepting of one's experiences in the present

By using fMRI measurements alongside MBSR, current literature has been able to show that interventions can actually alter connectivity networks in the brain. Over an eight-week period, women were assigned to an MBSR training course, and fMRI data were gathered at each step. The tasks performed showed evidence for increased functional connectivity within the auditory and visual networks and within the auditory cortex and attentional areas of the brain. The researchers concluded that MBSR may result in attentional focus, enhanced sensory processing, and more awareness of sensory experiences.[169]

Another well-cited research study used MRI results to determine how structural brain matter changes over time in the MBSR programs. The people in the study also underwent an eight-week program with MBSR interventions. The anatomical analyses indicated increases in gray matter concentration in the left hippocampus, the posterior cingulate cortex, and the cerebellum. [170] According to the researchers, these brain areas are highly involved in learning and memory processes as well as emotional regulation.

The current debates surrounding wellness programs focus on data and metrics on the benefits they have claimed. Different programs may illustrate extremely different results in terms of potential health benefits. Perhaps it is time to also

169 Marchand, William R. 2014. "Neural Mechanisms Of Mindfulness And Meditation: Evidence From Neuroimaging Studies". World Journal Of Radiology 6 (7): 471. doi:10.4329/wjr.v6.i7.471.

170 Ibid

focus on metrics that may be less directly evident, similar to the neuroimaging studies cited above.

## FUTURE-FORWARD:

### Stress Management Corporate Tips

For future research studies on wellness programs, cortisol level measurements and MRI scans may be one path to further understanding the impact wellness programs may have on brain health in the workforce. Rather than focusing solely on an economic perspective, more research is necessary to determine the full impact of wellness programs.

However, in the meantime, there are approaches to increase employee stress management skills.

1. Keep in mind that those around you learn by example. If you are a manager or an organization leader, make sure the manner in which you deal with your own stress reflects how you would want others in your organization to manage their stress.

2. Focus on an internal locus of control. The locus of control is how you perceive the degree to which you believe you have control over the outcome of events in your own life, as opposed to the degree to which external forces control the outcome of your life. Increasing your internal locus of control puts you in the driver's seat of the outcomes.

3. Learn about cognitive restructuring and mindfulness. Cognitive restructuring teaches one how to handle irrational thoughts, such as negative self-talk. It encourages you to change and modify those negative patterns. Mindfulness is a psychological tool for bringing one's active attention to the present moment.

### Accessibility to Wellness Programs

Another factor to consider is the accessibility of such programs. How do we ensure those who may not be in companies that provide such benefits also have a chance to practice healthy stress management for overall brain health?

For those who may not be in the corporate world, it is equally important to protect and manage stress. As Harvard Health Publishing states, stress management may reduce health problems linked to chronic cognitive issues and higher risks of Alzheimer's disease and dementia. If we find ourselves exposed to chronic stressors, it becomes important for us to individually take initiative and seek out evidence-based programs proven to decrease stress levels.

While there are MBSR programs offered usually at a high price, there are also existing resources online for free, such as a program under Jon Kabat-Zinn. Kabat-Zinn was a professor at the University of Massachusetts Medical School who promotes mindfulness meditation.[171] As a whole, it is amazing that the corporate world recognizes the negative consequences of stress on health and brain health.

### Actionable Ideas:

1. Regardless of where you are on your journey with brain health, one of the very first aspects to tackle along this journey is your stress level. Look up the Holmes-Rahe Stress Inventory. Where do you fall on the score?
2. In situations in which there are no opportunities or incentives to take responsibility and learn about stress

---

171 Kabat-Zinn, Jon. 2019. "Jon Kabat-Zinn: Defining Mindfulness – Mindful". Mindful.

management techniques, take it upon yourself to seek out resources for the sake of your brain.

3. Utilize online resources or courses that focus on mindfulness and stress reduction.

*As Jon Kabat-Zinn has stated, "Mindfulness practice means that we commit fully in each moment to be present; inviting ourselves to interface with this moment in full awareness, with the intention to embody as best we can an orientation of calmness, mindfulness, and equanimity right here and right now."* [172]

---

172  Ibid

# CHAPTER 12

# THE UPCOMING PHARMACEUTICAL DRUGS FOR THE BRAIN

———

*"[Humankind] is not going to wait passively for millions of years before evolution offers [us] a better brain."*

-DR. CORNELIU GIURGEA[173]

"Why are you finding internships that are unpaid?" I recall the direct conversations I had with my mother in my sophomore year. To be transparent, there were numerous opportunities I chose to pursue in college that came with a cost of my time and no compensation. As a brief reminder, there is an inherent value that can come with many experiences,

———

173 Giurgea, Corneliu E. 1982. "The Nootropic Concept And Its Prospective Implications". Drug Development Research 2 (5): 441-446. doi:10.1002/ddr.430020505.

as long as you ensure you can pinpoint your intentions and motivations going in.

Needless to say, after spending months interviewing and almost flying to Washington, DC for an unpaid summer internship, I was relieved to hear back from a pharmaceutical company in the Bay Area. The compensation, again, meant very little to me. What did matter was the irreplaceable understanding I have of the pharmaceutical industry. I interned at a company that's mission was to create cures for rare diseases, and its values were extremely patient-focused. Each of the conference rooms was named after patients who had been part of the clinical trials or who had received treatments.

As of today, I can truly appreciate the role of the pharmaceutical world, especially with the potential of drugs in improving health outcomes. Although the company I interned for was not focused on developing any therapeutics for brain health or neurological diseases, the prevalence of "brain-enhancing drugs" has been steadily increasing and is predicted to reach 5,959 million by 2024.

With that in mind, what exactly constitutes a brain-enhancing drug?

## THE FATHER OF NOOTROPICS

As with much of science, the discovery of nootropics was unintentional. In the 1960s, Romanian doctor Corneliu Giurgea was on a mission to create a motion sickness drug treatment. During his clinical trials, Giurgea was primarily researching the substance piracetam. Piracetam was a substance Giurgea had synthesized himself and spent hours in the lab refining as a drug for motion sickness. Much to his surprise, the results of the experiment demonstrated a greater trend. During the clinical trials, piracetam had notably increased the mental performance and memory consolidation of the research participants. Giurgea deemed mental enhancers as "nootropics," combining the Greek words "nous," which means "mind," and "tropein," which means "to bend." [174]

Following his discovery, Giurgea was quick to further outline what constitutes a nootropic. Essentially, these criteria suggested that nootropics enhanced cognition but also have brain-protecting properties.

His outlined criteria included:

   a. Enhancement of learning
   b. Enhance the brain's resistance to conditions of disruption
   c. Protect the brain from chemical or physical disruption
   d. Increased tonic cortico-subcortical control mechanisms
   e. Absence of pharmacological side effects of neuropsychotropic drugs.[175]

From the 1970s to the 1980s, nootropic development continued and entered mainstream society. Several other notable nootropic drugs developed during this time included aniracetam, currently used for Alzheimer's, and phenibut, which helps with anxiety and insomnia.

In recent decades, there has been increasing interest in nootropics as a "smart pill." This brain-booster may involve enhancing cognitive performance and increasing mental functions such as memory, motivation, attention, and creativity. The media attention on nootropics has grown as

---

174  Ibid

175  Ibid

more people are curious about nootropics' effects on normal cognition.

During the twentieth century, the FDA began to regulate the prescription-based nootropics.

## FDA REGULATION ON NOOTROPICS

Currently, there are few regulations on nootropics in the United States. The two primary forms of nootropics are dietary supplements and prescription drugs.

For nootropic dietary supplements, a lot of nootropic users directly regulate dosages, cycling, or usage completely based on forums online instead of actual medical or federal regulations. Many of the nootropics are regulated as "dietary supplements," which is in the same category as food regulations. The policy currently used considers nootropics in the form of dietary supplements legally "innocent" until proven to be negative for health. Herbs and extracts and some synthetic or semi-synthetic nootropic substances are also not regulated. Across the United States, the United Kingdom, Canada, and other countries, there are discrepancies in which nootropics are legal without prescription. For example, piracetam itself is legal to purchase and use in the United States and Canada without prescription but requires a prescription in the United Kingdom and Australia. These criteria vary based on location and the nootropic itself for many other drugs as well.

For prescription-based nootropics, there are two primary factors the FDA considers. Controlled nootropics require a prescription or an age verification to purchase. Scheduled nootropics are ranked by risk of abuse as a drug, with Schedule I as high risk and Schedule V as low risk. There are a few common pharmaceutical-based nootropics, such as Ritalin and Adderall, for attention-deficit/hyperactivity disorder (ADHD). A more recent drug, Modafinil, known to treat narcolepsy, is also considered a nootropic. People have linked the drug to benefits such as alertness, energy, focus, and decision-making. Unfortunately, a lot of prescribed medicine is illegally resold without a prescription.

## COMMONLY USED OR ABUSED PRESCRIBED NOOTROPICS

People have recently turned to Modafinil under the brand Provigil. There are supporters of this drug from some prominent individuals. However, this drug was created to boost "wakefulness" for people with sleep apnea or narcolepsy.

Modafinil is cited to increase alertness, energy, focus, and decision-making. It targets the dopaminergic pathways. When dopamine is released between synapses of neurons, there are usually transporters responsible for dopamine reuptake. These are called dopamine active transporters (DAT). Modafinil blocks DATs and enhances the amount of time dopamine is available as a neurotransmitter.

Adderall is very similar in its mechanisms except that it blocks the reuptake of several neurotransmitters, including norepinephrine, dopamine, and serotonin. It also serves to increase the release of these neurotransmitters in the synaptic area.

In 2006, up to 25 percent of college students reported having used stimulants for ADHD in the previous year, while only 4 to 7 percent reported diagnosis with ADHD. This misuse happens frequently, and I have witnessed such interactions in my own time at Berkeley. A lot of young students are naive to the legal repercussions. Sharing is not always caring. Trading of prescribed nootropics is an illegal act that constitutes a violation of federal and state drug trafficking laws. Distribution of amphetamines is punishable by up to five to twenty years in prison with a $250,000 to $5 million fine. If a defendant is convicted of selling drugs near a school, the penalty in both years and fine will double. I emphasize the legality, as the consequences should not be taken lightly.

Some people may criticize the strictness of these regulations. However, amphetamines also have health consequences. There are potential dangers in reselling prescription nootropics which, although temporarily appealing for those who want to utilize them, may have negative long-term effects.

Within the listed side effects, there is the loss of appetite, inability to fall or stay asleep, abnormal heartbeats, abdominal pains, and abnormal muscle movements. Side effects may also include elevated blood pressure, chest pain, shortness of breath, psychosis, and manic episodes. A study indicated that one in ten children placed on stimulants for ADHD develops psychotic symptoms, which are reversible with the withdrawal of the medication. The FDA has enforced warnings for Ritalin and Adderall, requiring the labels of these drugs to indicate an increased risk of sudden cardiac death.

## MOST COMMONLY-USED DIETARY NOOTROPICS

Several of the most commonly used nootropics not regulated by the FDA may come as a surprise. These are the most commonly utilized dietary nootropics.

### Caffeine

According to *Forbes*, Americans consume an average of 300 mg of caffeine per day, amounting to around three cups of coffee. Caffeine has psychoactive effects and is considered a nootropic. As many of us have directly noticed, caffeine increases alertness and improves attention. Caffeine also has been shown to improve performance on response times, information processing, and vigilance tasks. Molecularly, caffeine has the same structure as neuro mediators known as adenosine. In the brain, adenosine binds to receptors and slows down neural activities, facilitating sleep and dilating blood vessels. Instead, the caffeine blocks the receptors in the nervous system, so fewer adenosine molecules are able to bind to the receptors. Therefore, the adenosine processes such as facilitation of sleep or slowing of neural processes are delayed, leading to an increase in energy. Caffeine also increases the production of dopamine, a neurotransmitter related to motivation and reward.

## L-Theanine

L-theanine is a supplement found predominantly in tea, particularly green tea. L-theanine easily crosses the blood-brain barrier and enters the brain. EEG studies have shown that L-theanine at dosages higher than 200 mg modulates brain function by increasing alpha waves. Alpha brain waves between 8 to 12 Hz indicate a relaxation effect without drowsiness. L-theanine is also linked to an increase in neurotransmitters, including GABA, serotonin, and dopamine. Generally, L-theanine is believed to increase cognitive alertness and creativity.

## Panax Ginseng

Ginseng is a plant root that is commonly used in Chinese herbal medicine. Along with being an antioxidant, ginseng is known to be a neuroprotectant. The active components in the plant include ginsenosides. Research suggests ginseng may increase the rates of learning and help with cognitive enhancement. As a nootropic, ginseng improves working memory performance and reaction times.

### Ginkgo Biloba

Ginkgo biloba is a plant that has positive effects on the brain. A study in the Journal of Psychopharmacology examined the effects of ginkgo on dementia. Though research is limited still, the Mayo Clinic suggests only several small studies have shown cognitive improvements in memory in dementia patients. However, many of the larger studies have not confirmed the benefits of ginkgo.

Even with the most common nootropics, additional research is necessary before some of these substances can be truly promoted as brain-enhancing. Unfortunately, while there is validity in a few of the nootropic claims, there remain many exaggerated claims on the effects of these substances.

**FUTURE-FORWARD:**

### The Increasing Use of "Smart Drugs"

Nootropics, also known as smart drugs, consist of synthetic or natural substances used to improve mental performance in cognitively healthy individuals. As a result, these products are highly appealing to students of this generation who are taking exams or looking for mental boosts in a competitive environment.

The company Mind Lab Pro currently suggests its consumers include students who want to boost studying abilities, athletes who want to be their best in training, competitors in mental challenges such as poker, professionals who hope to stay driven in their careers, artists who need concentration to produce fantastic productions, and people older than fifty-five who want to maintain healthy cognition. Overall, this range of advertising is seen across most nootropic companies that hope to sell a large number of products to a wide demographic. Keep in mind, as stated in the paragraphs prior, that the FDA does not regulate dietary supplement products.

However, from a research or medical perspective, it is perhaps beneficial to examine who should or should not be engaged in nootropics. In 2016, the American Medical Association as a whole held a meeting over the concern of nootropics. As of June 2016, the AMA has adopted the policy of discouraging nonmedical use of prescription drugs for cognitive enhancement in healthy individuals. As the AMA emphasizes, prescription stimulants are not risk-free, nor do they make people smarter. This restriction requires that drugs for ADHD or narcolepsy not be sold to or used by people who do not have a proper prescription. The emphasis is on the idea that these drugs, as implicated prior, are not risk-free.

> "As temptation grows to use prescription drugs for a competitive advantage at work and school, the nonmedical use of these drugs should be discouraged given potential for substance misuse and other adverse consequences."

—DR. MAYA A. BABU[176]

---

176 "AMA Confronts The Rise Of Nootropics". 2019. American Medical Association.

As for the dietary supplements or botanical substances used or advertised for cognitive enhancement, the safety and efficacy have not been examined and require more systematic evaluation. In 2015, a meta-analysis of randomized controlled trials found that many of the nutritional ingredients advertised in dietary nootropic supplements have no real significance to cognition. Omega-3 fatty acids, B vitamins, and E vitamins were included in this study in the form of supplements.

While the study did not rule out the potential for nootropics to be beneficial at all, there was just not enough evidence to support the claims. As for the nootropic advertisements, the AMA has currently asked the Federal Trade Commission to evaluate the advertising for nootropics to ensure the proposed benefits are not misleading. There needs to be more research conducted on nootropics to have a better evidence-driven and regulation-based system.

### Ethics of Using Smart Drugs

While the interest in nootropics remains very high, a few ethical questions remain. As with prior chapters, there are issues of accessibility, peer-pressure, and risk.

Considering that pharmaceutical products and even supplemental products cost money, who will have the most access to these products? Essentially, the well-off will be financially able to buy nootropics first. In such a competitive world, there are definitely people with wealth who would let their children use nootropics in order to ensure their children perform well in school or during major tests or athletic events. A society that promotes nootropics creates barriers for those people without the financial means to purchase the drugs. To compare normal cognitive performance to that of nootropic-users may not result in fair evaluations.

Peer pressure is often cited as a reason for consuming nootropics. How do we mitigate the pressures of being a perfect student with impeccable intelligence? Should that competitive pressure overtake the potential negative effects of consuming nootropics?

The effects of pharmacological nootropics are not suggested to be completely safe, as side effects are risky. Moreover, researchers, medical professionals, pharmaceutical companies, and the FDA all need to collaborate to issue better regulations that outline more precisely the long-term effects of pharmaceutical nootropics.

Overall, you should imagine what type of environment you want to be in. What do you personally think about nootropics? What do you think about the effects of a society dependent on nootropics? As nootropics continue to grow in popularity, we need to be prepared to consider all the implications.

**Actionable Ideas:**
1. Think about these questions: What do you personally think about nootropics? What do you think about the effects of a society dependent on nootropics? How do you think inequality gaps may increase?
2. If or when you next encounter someone without a prescription using or offering Adderall, remember the implications, legal and health-wise.

*As stated by Simon Essig Aberg for the National Center for Health Research,*

*"The attitudes of parents, students, college administrators, and law enforcement towards Adderall and Ritalin abuse have been ambivalent; since they are used for studying, they are often assumed to be just a little different than caffeine. At the very least, students need to be aware of the serious risks that can occur; although the most serious are rare, that doesn't matter if it happens to you or someone you care about. Parents, health care professionals, counselors, and college administrators should be sure to include Adderall and other 'study drugs' in any conversation about the dangers of substance abuse."* [177]

<hr>

177 Research, National. 2019. "'Study Drug' Abuse By College Students: What You Need To Know | National Center For Health Research". National Center For Health Research.

# CHAPTER 13

# THE NEAR FUTURE OF MEDICALLY PRESCRIBED VIDEO GAME THERAPIES

"Video games rot your brains." That is one of the most frequently repeated mantras in today's society. In my earlier years, I, too, believed the use of technology and video games hindered cognitive abilities. Whenever my classmates spoke about *League of Legends* or the new fad games, I remained woefully oblivious. As I am sure many of us have experienced, my parents were consistently drilling in the idea that video games were just an addiction and a waste of time. When the Nintendo Wii came out, my parents caved and got my sister and me a console game. We were limited to an hour per week, during which we would play *Mario Kart, Wii Sports*, or *Cooking Mama*.

By the time I entered high school, I had grown out of the Wii and was no longer interested in video games. Regardless, the big YouTube gamers such as PewDiePie and gaming streamers became a huge fad during my high school years. I found it fascinating that performing digital feats or conquering challenges in a virtual world could be so satisfying for a lot of people in my generation.

Imagine my surprise when I found myself at the campus of the University of California, San Francisco approximately four years later, interviewing at a neuroscience lab focused specifically on the potential of video game therapeutics. During the interview, I was prompted to give instructions to a few cognitive exams. About a week later, I heard back from the lab interviewer and was offered an internship at the Neuroscape Lab. I was stoked, not only because this clinical interventional research was novel to me, but also because the lab was truly spearheading an entirely new movement in digital therapeutics.

From my junior to senior year at Berkeley, I had the opportunity to work in the Neuroscape Lab, which is headed by Dr. Adam Gazzaley. Gazzaley is a prominent neuroscientist and entrepreneur who completed his training at the Mount Sinai School of Medicine, followed by a residency at the University of Pennsylvania and post-doctoral training at Berkeley.

Contradictory to what one might imagine based on his background, Gazzaley's first entrepreneurial venture was a photography business. During Gazzaley's residency in internal medicine, Adam began his entrepreneurial journey with a company called Wanderings. Wanderings is a company that still exists today, through which Gazzaley sells prints of his own nature photography. Despite his interest in photography, Gazzaley's additional impressive pursuits set him up for success in other areas as well. As seen directly on

Wanderings' website, Gazzaley's website references *Decade 1: 1997-2006*, with a quote that follows:

"Not all those who wander are lost."



## AKILI INTERACTIVE AND THE NEUROSCAPE LAB

After creating his photography business, Gazzaley expanded his entrepreneurial path to the scientific world by founding the UCSF Neuroscape Lab in 2006. The lab focuses predominantly on designing and testing the foundations of novel brain assessments with the aim of impacting cognitive health and medicine through technology. Brain plasticity is a foundational focus within the lab. which evaluates how we can refine our behavior and elevate our minds.[178]

Can we refine our behavior and elevate our minds through technology?

The lab uses the strategy of closed-loop systems. A closed-loop system involves an intervention, followed by the rapid recording of the impact of the intervention. In terms of the custom-designed video games, the participants engage in the game, and the game records multiple variables of performance abilities. Immediately, the game engine provides adaptive feedback and shifts the difficulty of the game to challenge your current abilities.

Once the technologies are developed, they are placed into rigorous research studies that track and evaluate the impact they actually have on brain performance and brain

---

178 "Akili Interactive". 2019. Akili Interactive.

physiology. The primary methods of tracking brain progress are through neurophysiological tools such as fMRI, EEG, and TMS.

The video games are being used to test how factors such as attention, working memory, and goal management evolve as we age. In 2011, Gazzaley proposed the idea of a video game that would activate the prefrontal cortex and challenge the brain to improve function and cognitive abilities. After deliberating the feasibility, he reached out to LucasArts, a game design company, and created the game Adaptive Cognitive Evaluation (ACE) through collaboration.

In the five years the ACE program has been running, the results illustrate that certain cognitive functions, such as multitasking, decrease steadily from age twenty to eighty. This trend also occurs for other cognitive abilities we take for granted. With the impactful results of this study, Gazzaley became convinced there was a specific area of growth for video game interventions that targeted cognitive aging as well as cognitive diseases.[179]

Furthermore, the study opened the doors to exciting propositions on how technology can improve cognitive functions in medical diseases, such as attention for ADHD patients. Within the Gazzaley Lab, there are clinical trials hoping to transform video games into prescriptible FDA-approved therapeutics. Gazzaley is currently collaborating directly with Akili Interactive, which asks us to "Imagine what medicine can be." [180]

Akili Interactive was founded, with Gazzaley on the board of directors, in order to create a new class of prescription

---

179 Ibid

180 Ibid

digital medicines. The Neuroscape Lab is partnering closely with Akili for an ADHD intervention that has already entered the process of FDA-regulated clinical trials. Within the FDA regulations, the therapeutic tool will have to prove itself as useful as other drug-based therapeutics in the market for ADHD in order for physicians to be able to prescribe the video game as an alternative.

## "Imagine what medicine can be."

In 2018, Akili Interactive closed a $55 million funding round. Akili's best-known trial is AKL-T01, which consisted of 348 patients who were both children and adolescents diagnosed with ADHD. In just four weeks, AKL-T01 managed to show statistically significant improvement compared to the baseline psychiatric measures of attention levels. The next step is bringing this evidence to the FDA for the approval process.[181]

Neuroscape is also targeting several other conditions in its clinical program, including autism, depression, TBI, mild cognitive impairment, and dementia. In my past few years at the Neuroscape lab, I ran the ACE program on a weekly basis with participants over age sixty-five. While it is evident that the younger generation is excited for the merging potential of technology, virtual reality games, and brain health interventions, several of the older individuals I worked with had mixed opinions.

After playing the eleven games on ACE, a few older people told me, "Technology tires me out, that was way too much for me," while others responded much more positively about how

---

181  Ibid

it reminded them of the most recent iPad game they down-loaded. Given the idea that these video games are moving toward FDA-approved clinical trials, it is essential to consider who the target population is and whether one will be able to adhere to the intervention as easily as following a drug prescription.

## FDA REGULATION ON DIGITAL THERAPEUTICS

Now, what role does FDA regulation have on technology usage in the emerging era of digital therapeutics? To define a digital therapeutic (DTx) further, it consists of an evidence-based therapeutic intervention for patients driven by programs that prevent, manage, or treat a mental disorder or disease.

In September 2017, the FDA passed the first mobile medical application to treat substance use disorders. A substance use disorder is diagnostically under the category of psychological or mental disorders. It involves the recurrent use of alcohol and drugs to the point of functional impairment, including health and failure to meet basic responsibilities at school, work, or home. The mobile app is called Reset and was the first digital therapeutic to undergo the process of FDA approval. Within the app, there is a patient application and clinician dashboard, and it focuses on the method of CBT. The platform is intended to be used in conjunction with other treatments and utilizes built-in rewards and incentives for the patient to adhere to the program.

Under the company Novartis, the clinical trial for Reset involved 399 patients in a twelve-week, multisite program. At the end of the twelve weeks, the data proved the application was beneficial through its statistical significance in increasing abstinence from alcohol, cocaine, marijuana, and stimulants. The adherence rates revealed that 40.3 percent in the clinical trial stayed abstinent compared to 17.6 percent for the control group that did not engage in Reset. As of now, Reset is being marketed as a therapeutic device under Pear Therapeutics.

Abbott was also granted FDA clearance for a diabetes product known as FreeStyle LibreLink. This app, first available in Europe and now approved in the United States, allows users with diabetes to scan sensors with an app on their smartphones instead of using continuous glucose monitoring (CGM). CGM is most commonly used by Type 1 diabetics to track their glucose levels. Rather than a fingerstick method, the Freestyle Libre system allows a sensor worn on the back of the upper arm and app to check insulin levels. This new, FDA-approved device not only allows for more discretion and convenience when measuring glucose levels but also allows data to be uploaded directly into the platform known as LibreView for easier access of tracked data.

The products that enter the FDA's tough metrics of approval are validated in their effectiveness through data-driven measures. It is exciting to imagine the increasing number of FDA-approved digital therapeutics in the near future. Due to the fact that these products are now considered an FDA-approved therapy, the product is only available under prescription.

## GROWING INTEREST IN DIGITAL THERAPEUTICS

According to a report from PricewaterCoopers in 2019, 54 percent of surveyed users were open to trying a digital app or online tool approved by the FDA. Around 56 percent of physicians in the report have also brought up digital therapy as a potential therapeutic for patients. Big pharmaceutical companies have also been fairly interested in investing their funds in digital therapy solutions. Already between 2017 and 2018, investors poured around $12.5 billion into digital health ventures.

In 2026, the digital therapeutics market is expected to be at a compound annual growth rate of 21.6 percent. Although it seems as if interest is at an all-time high, there are still hesitations from consumers. While this may or may not be a large concern, it is the duty of the FDA moving forward to create the proper regulations to protect patient data under digital therapeutics.

In any setting, privacy is a large concern, and the measures used in standard forms of treatment may have to be amplified for digital therapeutics. According to research by Savvy Cooperative in 2018, one-third of the respondents feared devices and digital therapeutics may be tracking behavior invasively. Others are also worried data may be sold to third parties without permission.

The component of data privacy adds another layer to the puzzle. Not only do consumers or patients have to trust the therapeutics or interventions, but they also have to be able to trust the technology's security.

**FUTURE-FORWARD:**

### The Importance of Scientific Evidence for Medical Devices

In the midst of redefining medicine with digital therapeutics, how should we approach brain health technology that has no scientific backing through clinical trials?

In the recent decade since the beginning of the mobile app era, there has been a surge of brain health training companies. A lot of companies claim to have research backing on the improvements their apps have on cognitive function. However, without running proper clinical trials, it is difficult to properly pinpoint the exact changes that are occurring, so a lot of companies may be riding on unvalidated claims.

Luminosity is one of the most popular brain training apps in the market. Joaquin Anguera, a UCSF assistant professor of neurology, states that the modules possibly have positive effects on the brain but that thorough research is necessary to determine the exact benefits of each game. In one specific study, the researchers recruited 128 young adults and separated the adults into two groups: one that played video games for ten weeks straight and one that used the Luminosity app for ten weeks straight. Baseline cognitive tests were taken before and after the ten-week study.

Researchers discovered no statistically significant differences in cognitive improvement between the two groups. A third group engaged in no activities, acting as the control group. This group's results were similar to that of the experimental groups. One major potential issue with applications like Luminosity is the lack of knowledge on which neural circuits are targeted and which cognitive deficits are being addressed in each module. Therefore, it is important to tread carefully with unregulated digital health apps because, without official clinical trials, the functionality and usefulness of products may be unclear.

Besides companies or research organizations that focus on digital therapeutics, clinics are also taking a stab at being involved in the world of digital therapeutic interventions. In April 2019, a start-up in Palo Alto, California received $4.2 million in seed funding. Meru Health is a digital twelve-week intervention program in which users have access to therapists virtually. The users also have access to anonymous support groups targeting depression and anxiety.

The journal *Nature* discovered in March 2019 that most mental health apps were not evidence-based or peer-reviewed. Researchers found that only around 14 percent included any evidence of benefits, while 64 percent claimed efficacy without any proof of their claims. Researchers identified 1,435 mental health apps, screened around 350 as a sample, and used seventy-three in the final analysis. "There are a lot of opportunities for patients to receive bad care through apps right now. It is very important that it is evidence-based care and not given by unlicensed clinicians, or given by a job coach or someone who really wants to give advice, but rather someone that has training and has patient experience," Jennifer Gentile from Ieso Digital Health said.

Meru Health, on the other hand, has paired with Stanford's School of Medicine and VA Palo Alto Health Care System researchers to determine the efficacy of digital therapeutic platforms like this one. There are perceived benefits of digital applications and platforms for mental health. Primarily, the benefits involve accessibility of real-time remote health care professionals and care accountability. From Meru Health's perspective, digital therapeutic interventions can also aim to encourage patients to feel more empowered and engaged in their own treatment. An eight-week program was launched between March and December 2017 that consisted of 141 participants. The results showed 86 percent of people completed the full treatment program and around 75 percent of people showed a 20 percent reduction in depressive symptoms. More research is being conducted by Meru Health to satisfy the evidence-based approach for digital therapeutics.

### Access for Digital Therapies

As with many other medicines, there is a genuine concern that prescription medications may often be less accessible. In a 2010 study on prescription drug accessibility, Steven Morgan and Ja Kennedy found that Americans are more likely to use prescription drugs than are residents of other countries, including the United Kingdom, Australia, Canada, and Germany among others. However, Americans were also more likely to experience financial barriers in accessing medications and paid more out of pocket for prescriptions. Along with that, the research showed that the United States has larger income-based inequities in relation to pharmaceutical use. In relation to digital therapeutics that will also be prescription-based, accessibility is one concern that needs to be further addressed.

From the pharmaceutical perspective, profit from a product is undeniably a goal for companies. According to consulting firm Simon-Kucher, several suggested methods of monetizing digital therapeutics include[182]:

A) Traditional pharmaceutical or medical reimbursement. This requires insurance plans may be able to reimburse therapeutics, similarly to the process of prescribed drugs.

B) Offer multiple versions or a customized offering of the digital therapeutic. This method requires that the company may produce "lite" versions of the therapeutics that are available to be purchased with cash, while the normal versions require insurance coverage and prescriptions.

As seen in these models, the patient who desires to use these products either needs insurance or available cash. One

---

182 Lee, David. "Monetizing Digital Therapeutics." Simon Kucher & Partners.

consideration is how to make these digital therapeutics accessible to those without insurance while maintaining the same versions instead of opting for "lite" versions that may not provide all the functions available. Either way, the financial and accessibility issues will have to be addressed in the near future when more digital therapeutics are approved.

**Actionable Ideas:**
1. Scroll through brain training apps on your phone. Search up the ones you have on Google. Which of these have an evidence-based approach?
2. Look up evidence-based approach apps surrounding mental health or brain training. Consider which of these would you be interested in using.

The integration of credible technology therapeutics into medicine is an exciting development. Keep in mind that digital therapeutics as a whole and, more specifically for the brain, are upcoming areas of interest that have some promising potential for several neurological and psychiatric diseases. As listed on Gazzaley's photography business mentioned earlier, he quotes this under *Decade 2: 2007-2016*:

*"Traveler, there is no path.*
*The path is made by walking."*

—ANTONIO MACHADO[183]

---

183 Gazzaley, Adam. 2019. "Wanderings: Adam Gazzaley Photography". Smugmug.Com.

# CHAPTER 14

# THE BENEFITS OF SOCIAL MEDIA FOR A BRAIN ADVOCACY MOVEMENT

—

*"We're living at a time when attention is the new currency. Those who insert themselves into as many channels as possible look set to capture the most value."*

–PETE CASHMORE[184]

#Inspiration. #Motivation. #Medicine. A couple of months ago, I was browsing through my Instagram "Explore" page without expecting to discover anything novel when I came

---

184 Pete Cashmore Quote: "We're Living At A Time When Attention Is The New Currency. Those Who Insert Themselves Into As Many Channels As Possible...". 2019. Quotefancy.Com.

across those exact hashtags. Even with my interest in medicine, I had been oblivious to the fact that this whole other realm of social media existed on this social media platform. Continuing into the rabbit hole of these hashtags, I landed on Dr. Cat Begovic's page @beautybydrcat. Her name rang a bell.

In summer 2016, I spent the entire three months interning at 77 Plastic Surgery under Dr. Larry Fan. One of my primary tasks was to explore how the top-followed plastic surgeons marketed themselves and how to use Instagram as a platform to engage potential consumers and patients. Within this project, I examined the Instagram of several physicians in the process as a reference point. One of the prominent physicians within the intersection of medicine and social media is Dr. Catherine Begovic.

## THE INSTAGRAM DOCTOR

Begovic currently holds around 1.2 million followers on Instagram's platform alone. As a person who identifies most as a surgeon, Begovic is also the first of her kind as an "Instagram celebrity doctor." Most people in the medical community focus on making their impact in the classical sense by seeing patients and supporting patients in clinical settings. Begovic has been approaching her practice in a manner that has set an example for many others in the field of medicine.

From an early age, tenacity was the quality that Begovic demonstrated through her education and her career decisions. Throughout her whole career, Begovic was told again and again that, "Girls like you don't become doctors." Despite the criticism, Begovic found success at Harvard, which she credited to her high expectations of herself. Begovic has stated that "It's a long, hard road to become a surgeon — for anyone. It was challenging being one of the only women in my program. I demanded the highest performance of myself and that allowed me to earn the respect of my colleagues." [185]

Although Begovic is best known as a plastic surgeon in Los Angeles, the truth is she has also taken on the role of a social media influencer physician. Prior to Begovic's presence on social media, there was little to no presence of nurses, physician assistants, or physicians sharing their knowledge and experiences within the medical field on social media. What Begovic started was revolutionary: a new outlook on what social media could accomplish for influencers that may look to educate.

On a day to day basis, Begovic posts a lot of informational stories, patient testimonials, and consented videos of surgical procedures to her Instagram page. It gets a lot of attention—around two hundred comments and twenty thousand likes on each post. While she also shares motivational tips for those pursuing medicine, Begovic has illustrated that her page serves as a primary source of information for patients who may be considering procedures.

With this model of utilizing social media, #medicine now has around six million relevant posts on Instagram. Instagram became a new and effective way of not only sharing lifestyle pictures but also for medically trained individuals to share useful information. Plastic surgeons, in particular, have been extremely successful in engaging with this platform. Looking up the hashtag #plasticsurgeon—there are more than 700,000 results, whereas the hashtag #neurologist returns less than thirty-five thousand results.

---

185 "Catherine Huang-Begovic, M.D.". 2019. Medelita.

## BRAIN HEALTH ADVOCACY IN SOCIAL MEDIA

Perhaps these numbers indicate that certain specialties have not begun to engage with the tools at hand to inform potential patients and the broader community outside of their direct clinic and patients. The dissemination of research, as we have explored, is frequently a slow process, and even general medical information may not be common knowledge. Regardless of the harms of social media, definite benefits include reaching a larger audience. People who are working within the realm of brain health and maintenance should begin to consider how their platforms such as Instagram could infiltrate public awareness and knowledge of brain health. Who, then, is responsible for distributing brain health information to society?

Parkinson's Global Project sought to accomplish precisely that. The 501c3 nonprofit is dedicated to funding Parkinson's disease research and supporting Parkinson's associations around the world. Regardless of its following in terms of numbers, the group has done a commendable job of using social media to inform the public through Instagram. For example, one of the posts states that "The BEST known method of slowing disease progression via exercise is CARDIO which creates BDNF and gets oxygen and blood to the brain." Many other similar videos are informative and educational. The group has also uploaded clips of its workshops and specific movement demonstrations that are beneficial for Parkinson's patients.

Declare the past,
Diagnose the present,
Foretell the future.

Before attempting to move forward with an educational social media account, it is also necessary to remember that the Hippocratic Oath honors patient privacy. Currently, the social media of the cosmetic industry often illustrates patient before and after photos, as well as videos of the physical surgeries on both Snapchat and Instagram. While the videos are informative, this movement may be somewhat controversial for patient privacy. For health issues for which you cannot seek surgical enhancements, it is absolutely essential that patients are able to trust and rely on the fact that their health conditions are not broadcasted on social media in that manner.

Another aspect to consider for brain health in particular that differs from the cosmetic surgery industry is that cosmetic surgery is easily construed as a profitable business. While brain health organizations and clinics may be profitable, it is ethically questionable for neurologists and physicians within the brain health community to utilize social media as a marketing tool. Instead, approaching social media as an educational and potentially preventive opportunity aligns much more with the lines in the Hippocratic Oath, "I will remember that I do not treat a fever chart, a cancerous growth, but a sick human being, whose illness may affect the person's family and economic stability. My responsibility includes these related problems, if I am to care adequately for the sick. I will prevent disease whenever I can, for prevention is preferable to cure."

## FUTURE-FORWARD:

### Navigating Fake Health News

As of 2019, Dr. Austin Chiang was appointed as the first chief medical social media officer at his hospital. Chiang is a Harvard-trained gastroenterologist who also found himself as a prominent figure on Instagram. He is known as the "GI Doctor," with more than twenty thousand followers at the moment. While he shares selfies and photos, most of his captions indicate the latest research and provide real information to eliminate rumors on health. In Chiang's opinion, "This is the biggest crisis we have right now in health care. Everyone should be out there, but I realize I'm one of the few." [186]

As Chiang stated, most people who are not in the medical community do not read or pay close attention to medical journals or scientific literature. Globally, the average person spent around 136 minutes per day on social media in 2018. Working with this idea in mind, Chiang started recruiting people into the movement from his home hospital, Jefferson Health. He created a team of physicians that hopes to quell the inaccurate health content that is often spread across social media in rapid succession.

In order to recruit individuals to help him with the cause, Chiang created the Association for Healthcare Social Media. The organization consists of health professionals and

---

186 Chiang, Austin. 2019. "PRESS — Dr. Austin Chiang, MD MPH". Dr. Austin Chiang, MD MPH.

is actively working to create a set of guidelines on how health professionals should engage with digital social media tools.

Having physicians and accredited medical groups who are willing to take on the role of disseminating quality information through social media allows those who may not have immediate access to neurologists, neuropsychiatrists, or behavioral therapists to benefit from being better informed. If by chance you fit one of those categories as a neurologist or a health provider in a similar field, consider whether being an influencer in this manner could potentially align with your life vision as a physician.

In consideration of effectively reaching a large audience, there are plenty of social media resources one can further explore. Becoming an influencer involves learning the art of when to post, what to post, who to post to, and details I will leave up to professional social media strategists to illustrate. As long as the ethics and motivation as a physician are kept at the forefront, social media can be a useful tool for brain health advocacy.

**Actionable Ideas:**
1. If you are on social media, make sure the sources you are getting health information from are credible.
2. If you work in a field related to brain health, consider creating a social media platform to disseminate accurate brain health information to the public.

*As Chiang states, "With every single field out there, there's something that is misinterpreted or misconstrued by the general public. We want to meet the patient where they are."* [187]

---

187 Ibid

# CHAPTER 15

# THE FINAL FUTURE-FORWARD FOR YOU

—

*"Neuroscience is by far the most fascinating branch of science because the brain is the most fascinating object in the universe. Every human brain is different- the brain makes each human unique and defines who he or she is."*

—STANLEY B. PRUSINER[188]

Within the pages of this book, you have read inspiring stories of people who have brought forth great changes within the brain health sector. Together, we have explored a generous number of topics that surround the history, present, and future of our society's brain health. Moreover, the interplay of public health, research, and medical communities

---

188 Prusiner, Stanley. 2019. "Stanley B. Prusiner Quotes – Brainyquote".

Brainyquote.

will continue to be key. There have been fascinating new approaches in all fields regarding brain injuries, mental health, strokes, brain tumors, and neurodegenerative diseases.

As I have been emphasizing in the book, the responsibility does not end with professionals.

a) Take charge of what you can do for your own brain health. There are actions that improve the status of the brain, such as changes in physical activity and diet. Continue to work on lowering your risk of brain diseases by understanding high risks, such as blood pressure for strokes or environmental toxins for brain tumors. Start to question what health means to you. Does your image of health include brain health? If not, how can you incorporate healthy brain choices and behaviors, such as mindfulness?

b) Continue exploring and learning about brain health. I encourage you to keep up with validated research on these topics as promising new developments emerge. There is information out there. It is up to you to discern the validity of what you come across on the Internet or what is advertised to you as promising products for the mind. There are plenty more topics to explore from a biological and advocacy, including Lou Gehrig's disease (ALS), seizures, Parkinson's, and so many more rare disease. I apologize if I have not covered a specific topic of interest to you, but this book is the starting point and only the tip of the iceberg of an extensive wealth of knowledge you can gain.

c) Engage in brain health advocacy. Seize the upcoming opportunities that present themselves to you, whether that be helping with events for nonprofits or becoming a neurologist helping with Chiang's social media cause. In hearing several personal stories of those people who have endured brain diseases, I hope you have been inspired to engage with the lives of those affected. I impart to you the motto I live by:

I will forever strive toward a positive impact, no matter how small my contributions are, as they will feed into the momentum for greater change.

And my friends, I wish you all the best in your paths to understanding and adventuring into your journey within brain health. Be a #neuroadvocate.

# APPENDIX

---


2019. Epa.Gov.

@ErinWayman, Follow. 2019. "Louis Leakey: The Father Of Hominid Hunting". Smithsonian.

"04.12.2006 - Ethiopian Fossils Link Ape-Men With Earlier Hominids". 2019. Berkeley.Edu.

"A Neurosurgeon'S Guide To Sports-Related Head Injury". 2019. Aans.Org.

Aarli, Johan, Taran Dua, Aleksandar Janca, and Anna Muscetta. 2008. "Neurological Disorders: Public Health Challenges". Archives Of Neurology 65 (1): 154. doi:10.1001/archneurol.2007.19.

"About Proposition 65 - OEHHA". 2019. Oehha.Ca.Gov.

"About Us | JAPANESE SOCIETY OF NEUROLOGY". 2019. Neurology-Jp.Org.

"Adolescent Development Research And Its Impact On Health Policy". 2019. Unicef-Irc.Org.

Agnvall, Elizabeth. 2019. "New Survey: Americans Say Brain Health Is Crucial, But Protection Is Challenging". Blog: American Association Of Retired Persons.

"Akili Interactive". 2019. Akili Interactive.

"Alzheimer's Disease Fact Sheet". 2019. National Institute On Aging.

"Alzheimer's Patients May Face Looming Shortage Of Neurologists - Medicinenet". 2019. Medicinenet.

"AMA Confronts The Rise Of Nootropics". 2019. American Medical Association.

"American Brain Tumor Association". 2019. American Brain Tumor Association.

"American Congress Of Rehabilitation Medicine - An Overview | Sciencedirect Topics". 2019.

"An Interview With Marilyn Price Spivak | Brainline". 2019. Brainline.

"Ardipithecus Ramidus". 2019. The Smithsonian Institution's Human Origins Program.

Artico, Marco, Marialuisa Spoletini, Lorenzo Fumagalli, Francesca Biagioni, Larisa Ryskalin, Francesco Fornai, Maurizio Salvati, Alessandro Frati, Francesco Saverio Pastore, and Samanta Taurone.

2017. "Egas Moniz: 90 Years (1927–2017) From Cerebral Angiography". Frontiers In Neuroanatomy 11. doi:10.3389/fnana.2017.00081.

Banniester, Roger. 2019. "Roger Bannister Quotes". Brainyquote.

Berti, V., R.S. Osorio, L. Mosconi, Y. Li, S. De Santi, and M.J. de Leon. 2010. "Early Detection Of Alzheimer'S Disease With PET Imaging". Neurodegenerative Diseases 7 (1-3): 131-135. doi:10.1159/000289222.

"Bill Viola Quotes". 2019. Brainyquote.

"Brain Development - First Things First". 2019. First Things First.

"Brain Health". 2019. American Heart Association.

"Brenda Eskenazi". 2019. University Of California Research.

Burns, David D. 2012. Feeling Good. [Place of publication not identified]: HarperCollins.

"Cajal". 2019. Psu.Edu.

Camandola, Simonetta, and Mark P Mattson. 2017. "Brain Metabolism In Health, Aging, And Neurodegeneration". The EMBO Journal 36 (11): 1474-1492. doi:10.15252/embj.201695810.

"Cancer Statistical Facts". 2019. Cancer.Org.

Casper, S. T. 2010. "A Revisionist History Of American Neurology". Brain 133 (2): 638-642. doi:10.1093/brain/awp339.

"Catherine Huang-Begovic, M.D.". 2019. Medelita.

"Central Brain Tumor Registry Of The United States - NORD (National Organization for Rare Disorders)". 2019. NORD (National Organization for Rare Disorders).

"CHAMACOS Study | CERCH". 2019. Cerch.Berkeley.Edu.

Cheever, Laura W. 2014. "Transforming The Health Care Workforce Through Partnerships". Academic Medicine 89 (Supplement): S8. doi:10.1097/acm.0000000000000356.

Chiang, Austin. 2019. "PRESS — Dr. Austin Chiang, MD MPH". Dr. Austin Chiang, MD MPH.

Choi, Charles. 2019. "How Neanderthals Got Their Unusually Large Brains". Livescience.Com.

Collins, Thomas R. 2017. "Neurologic Diseases Found To Be The Largest Cause Of Disability Worldwide". Neurology Today 17 (22): 1. doi:10.1097/01.nt.0000527316.80068.88.

"Common Genetic Factors Found In 5 Mental Disorders". 2019. National Institutes Of Health (NIH).

"Conversation With Tim White, P. 2 Of 6". 2019. Globetrotter. Berkeley.Edu.

"DANA Foundation". 2019. Dana.Org.

"Decade Of The Brain Home Page (Library Of Congress)". 2019. Loc.Gov.

"Deepak Chopra Quote: "The Brain Has A Quality Referred To As Plasticity. The Ability To Form New Neural Pathways Even Into Very Old Age. The B...."". 2019. Quotefancy.Com.

Du, F., X.-H. Zhu, Y. Zhang, M. Friedman, N. Zhang, K. Ugurbil, and W. Chen. 2008. "Tightly Coupled Brain Activity And Cerebral ATP Metabolic Rate". Proceedings Of The National Academy Of Sciences 105 (17): 6409-6414. doi:10.1073/pnas.0710766105.

"Early Cancer Diagnosis Saves Lives, Cuts Treatment Costs". 2019. Who.Int.

"EPA's Position On The Effect Of Airborne Lead". 2019. Www3. Epa.Gov.

Fallon, Ivan. 2019. "Interview: Vitality Boss Adrian Gore Is In For The Long Run". Thetimes.Co.Uk.

Farah, Martha. 2019. "Mind, Brain And Education In Socioeconomic Context". Center For Cognitive Neuroscience.

"FDA Clears Vizai'S App To Detect And Notify Potential Stroke - Verdict Medical Devices". 2019. Verdict Medical Devices.

"First 5 California". 2019. First5california.Com. http://www.first-5california.com.

Furlong, Melissa A., Stephanie M. Engel, Dana Boyd Barr, and Mary S. Wolff. 2014. "Prenatal Exposure To Organophosphate Pesticides And Reciprocal Social Behavior In Childhood". Environment International 70: 125-131. doi:10.1016/j.envint.2014.05.011.

Gale, Seth. 2019. "Brain Healthy Behaviors Aid Patients With MCI, Mild Dementia". Medscape.

Gazzaley, Adam. 2019. "Photo Sharing. Your Photos Look Better Here.". Smugmug.Com.

"George Burns Quotes". 2019. Brainyquote.

"Get The Lead Out | U.S. PIRG". 2019. Uspirg.Org.

Giurgea, Corneliu E. 1982. "The Nootropic Concept And Its Prospective Implications". Drug Development Research 2 (5): 441-446. doi:10.1002/ddr.430020505.

"Glasgow Coma Scale". 2019. Cdc.Gov.

Gochfeld, Michael, and Joanna Burger. 2011. "Disproportionate Exposures In Environmental Justice And Other Populations: The Importance Of Outliers". American Journal Of Public Health 101 (S1): S53-S63. doi:10.2105/ajph.2011.300121.

Greicius, Julie. 2019. "'And Yet, You Try'". Stanford Medicine.

Habermann, Barbara. 2001. "Decade Of Behavior Follows The Decade Of The Brain". Journal Of Neuroscience Nursing 33 (2): 117. doi:10.1097/01376517-200104000-00011.

Hahnemann, Samuel. 2019. "Samuel Hahnemann Quotes". Brainyquote.

"Hardships Often Prepare Ordinary People For An Extraordinary Destiny. -C.S. Lewis - Google Search". 2019. Brainyquotes.

Harley, Kim G., Katherine Kogut, Daniel S. Madrigal, Maritza Cardenas, Irene A. Vera, Gonzalo Meza-Alfaro, and Jianwen She et al. 2016. "Reducing Phthalate, Paraben, And Phenol Exposure From Personal Care Products In Adolescent Girls: Findings From The HERMOSA Intervention Study". Environmental Health Perspectives 124 (10): 1600-1607. doi:10.1289/ehp.1510514.

"Healthychildren.Org - From The American Academy Of Pediatrics". 2019. Healthychildren.Org.

"Historical Overview | American Neurological Association (ANA)". 2019. Myana.Org.

"History Of Kessler Institute For Rehabilitation". 2019. Kessler-Rehab.Com.

Hodel, Amanda S. 2018. "Rapid Infant Prefrontal Cortex Development And Sensitivity To Early Environmental Experience". Developmental Review 48: 113-144. doi:10.1016/j.dr.2018.02.003.

Hofman, Michel A. 2014. "Evolution Of The Human Brain: When Bigger Is Better". Frontiers In Neuroanatomy 8. doi:10.3389/fnana.2014.00015.

"Homepage - Acquired Brain Injury Ireland". 2019. Acquired Brain Injury Ireland.

"How Tissue Plasminogen Activator (Tpa) Works For Stroke". 2019. Verywell Health.

"How Tissue Plasminogen Activator (Tpa) Works For Stroke". 2019. Verywell Health.

"How Virtual Reality Is Helping Special Tree Treat TBI | Special Tree". 2019. Specialtree.Com.

"Huffpost Is Now A Part Of Verizon Media". 2019. Huffpost.Com.

"Journal Of Neurology, Neurosurgery, And Psychiatry | JNNP'S Ambition Is To Publish The Most Ground-Breaking And Cutting-Edge Research From Around The World.". 2019. Journal Of Neurology, Neurosurgery, And Psychiatry.

Kabat-Zinn, Jon. 2019. "Jon Kabat-Zinn: Defining Mindfulness - Mindful". Mindful.

Kentner, Amanda C., Kelly G. Lambert, Anthony J. Hannan, and S. Tiffany Donaldson. 2019. "Editorial: Environmental Enrichment: Enhancing Neural Plasticity, Resilience, And Repair". Frontiers In Behavioral Neuroscience 13. doi:10.3389/fnbeh.2019.00075.

Kumar, D. R., F. Aslinia, S. H. Yale, and J. J. Mazza. 2010. "Jean-Martin Charcot: The Father Of Neurology". Clinical Medicine & Research 9 (1): 46-49. doi:10.3121/cmr.2009.883.

Kumar, K Suresh, Selvaraj Samuelkamaleshkumar, Anand Viswanathan, and Ashish S Macaden. 2019. "Cognitive Rehabilitation For Adults With Traumatic Brain Injury To Improve Occupational Outcomes."

Laskow, Sarah. 2019. "The Role Of The Supernatural In The Discovery Of Eegs". The Atlantic.

"Lead Poisoning: A Historical Perspective | About EPA | US EPA". 2019. Archive.Epa.Gov.

Lee, David. "Monetizing Digital Therapeutics." Simon Kucher & Partners.

"Lessons Learned In Decadal Planning". 2019. Sites.Nationalacademies.Org.

"Loveyourbrain". 2019. Loveyourbrain.

Marchand, William R. 2014. "Neural Mechanisms Of Mindfulness And Meditation: Evidence From Neuroimaging Studies". World Journal Of Radiology 6 (7): 471. doi:10.4329/wjr.v6.i7.471.

Marshall, Louise H, and Horace Winchell Magoun. 2010. Discoveries In The Human Brain. Totowa, N.J.: Humana Press.

"Martha J. Farah, Phd – Center For Neuroscience & Society". 2019. Neuroethics.Upenn.Edu.

"Mental Health By The Numbers | NAMI: National Alliance On Mental Illness". 2019. Nami.Org.

"Minamata Disease » Sustainability » Boston University". 2019. Bu.Edu.

Mosconi, Lisa. 2019. "About Dr. Lisa Mosconi — Lisa Mosconi, Phd". Lisa Mosconi, Phd.

Mosconi, Lisa. n.d. Brain Food. Avery/ Penguin Random House.

Mosconi, Lisa. 2019. "Exploring The Link Between Menopause And Alzheimer'S". Medium.

Naghavi, Mohsen. 2019. "Global, Regional, And National Burden Of Suicide Mortality 1990 To 2016: Systematic Analysis For The Global Burden Of Disease Study 2016". BMJ, l94. doi:10.1136/bmj.l94.

"National Institute Of Neurological Disorders And Stroke | National Institute Of Neurological Disorders And Stroke". 2019. Ninds.Nih.Gov.

"NCAA Publications - 2018-2019 NCAA Division I Manual - AUGUST VERSION - Available August 2018". 2019. Ncaapublications.Com.

Nelson, Calley, and PhD Samuel Mackenzie. 2019. "High-Tech Mouth Guards Raise Awareness Of Concussion Prevention". Everydayhealth.Com.

"Neurovr Neurosurgical Simulator | CAE Healthcare". 2019. Caehealthcare.Com.

"New Strategies And Approaches Needed To Cope With Growing Burden Of Brain Diseases". 2019. Eurekalert!.

"NIMH » Home". 2019. Nimh.Nih.Gov.

"Only 23% Of Americans Get Enough Exercise, A New Report Says". 2019. Time.Com.

Pearce, J M. 1997. "Johann Jakob Wepfer (1620-95) And Cerebral Haemorrhage.". Journal Of Neurology, Neurosurgery & Psychiatry 62 (4): 387-387. doi:10.1136/jnnp.62.4.387.

Pearce, Kevin. 2019. "Kevin Pearce - TED Talk". Youtube.Com.

Pearce, Kevin. 2019. "Kevin Pearce Is An American Snowboarder, Aspiring Sports Commentator And Advocate for The National Down Syndrome Society And The Prevention Of Traumatic Brain Injuries.". Kevinpearce.Com.

"Pete Cashmore Quote: "We'Re Living At A Time When Attention Is The New Currency. Those Who Insert Themselves Into As Many Channels As Possible...".". 2019. Quotefancy.Com.

"Physical Activity Resources". 2019. HHS.Gov.

Picard, Ken. 2019. "Kevin Pearce, Former Pro Snowboarder And TBI Survivor, Rises Again". Seven Days.

"President's Council On Sports, Fitness & Nutrition (PCSFN)". 2019. HHS.Gov.

Prusiner, Stanley. 2019. "Stanley B. Prusiner Quotes - Brainyquote". Brainyquote.

Psych, Mental. 2019. "Clinical Neuropsychologist Phoenix | Mental Edge Psych". John DenBoer. http://www.mentaledgepsych.com.

"Public Health Quotes - 10 Quotes On Public Health Science Quotes - Dictionary Of Science Quotations And Scientist Quotes". 2019. Todayinsci.Com.

"Publications And Resources". 2019. California Childcare Health Program.

Publishing, Harvard. 2019. "Exercise Can Boost Your Memory And Thinking Skills - Harvard Health". Harvard Health.

"Quickstats:Percentage* Of Adults† Aged ≥65 Years Meeting 2008 Federal Guidelines For Leisure-Time Aerobic§ And Muscle-Strengthening¶ Activities, By Age And Type Of Activity — United States, 2000–2002 And 2013–2015". 2016. MMWR. Morbidity And Mortality Weekly Report 65 (37): 1019. doi:10.15585/mmwr.mm6537a9.

Raghavan, Preeti. 2015. "Upper Limb Motor Impairment After Stroke". Physical Medicine And Rehabilitation Clinics Of North America 26 (4): 599-610. doi:10.1016/j.pmr.2015.06.008.

"RAND Corporation Provides Objective Research Services And Public Policy Analysis". 2019.

Ranpura, Ashish. 2019. "A Conversation With Marian Diamond - Brain Connection". Brain Connection.

Rauh, Virginia A., and Amy E. Margolis. 2016. "Research Review: Environmental Exposures, Neurodevelopment, And Child Mental Health - New Paradigms For The Study Of Brain And Behavioral Effects". Journal Of Child Psychology And Psychiatry 57 (7): 775-793. doi:10.1111/jcpp.12537.

Reference, Genetics. 2019. "Li-Fraumeni Syndrome". Genetics Home Reference.

Research, National. 2019. ""Study Drug" Abuse By College Students: What You Need To Know | National Center For Health Research". National Center for Health Research.

Rowland, Lewis P. 2003. NINDS At 50. New York: Demos Medical Pub., LLC.

Sanders, Robert. 2019. "Marian Diamond, Known For Studies Of Einstein'S Brain, Dies At 90". Berkeley News.

Sanders, Robert. 2019. "Marian Diamond, Known For Studies Of Einstein'S Brain, Dies At 90". Berkeley News.

"Sanjiv Sam Gambhir, MD, Phd, Receives 2018 Benedict Cassen Prize For Research In Molecular Imaging - SNMMI". 2019. Snmmi.Org.

"Sfn Expands Advocacy Efforts To Amplify Need For Funding". 2019. Sfn.Org.

"Sherwin B. Nuland, Author Of 'How We Die,' Is Dead At 83". 2019. Nytimes.Com.

"SMART Brain Aging". 2019. Smartbrainaging.Com. http://www.smartbrainaging.com.

Spitzer, Manfred. 2008. "Decade Of The Mind". Philosophy, Ethics, And Humanities In Medicine 3 (1): 7. doi:10.1186/1747-5341-3-7.

"Stanford Researchers Study Head Hits In High School Athletes". 2019. Mercurynews.Com.

Stocchetti, Nino, Giuseppe Citerio, Andrew Maas, Peter Andrews, and Graham Teasdale. 2008.

"Stress in America: The State of Our Nation. Stress in America Survey." *PsycEXTRA Dataset*, 2017.

"Bryan Jennett And The Field Of Traumatic Brain Injury. His Intellectual And Ethical Heritage In Neuro-Intensive Care". Intensive Care Medicine 34 (10): 1774-1778. doi:10.1007/s00134-008-1168-7.

"Stroke Death Rates, Total Population 35 And Older | Cdc.Gov". 2019. Cdc.Gov.

"Study Suggests 60% Of U.S. Neurologists Experiencing Burnout". 2019. Aan.Com.

Suzuki, Wendy. 2019. "Wendy Suzuki | Speaker | TED". Ted.Com.

Taylor, Jill. 2019. "My Stroke Of Insight". Ted.Com.

"TBI Research Review: Return To Work After Traumatic Brain Injury | Brainline". 2019. Brainline.

"TBI: Get The Facts | Concussion | Traumatic Brain Injury | CDC Injury Center". 2019. Cdc.Gov.

"The DANA Foundation, - Google Search". 2019. Google.Com.

"The Doctor Won'T See You Now? Study: US Facing A Neurologist Shortage". 2019. Aan.Com.

"The History Of Inhumane Mental Health Treatments | Talkspace". 2019. Talkspace.

"Tim D. White | American Paleoanthropologist". 2019. Encyclopedia Britannica.

Tonsaker, Tabitha. 2016. "Gold Mine Or Minefield?". New Scientist 231 (3084): 5. doi:10.1016/s0262-4079(16)31341-0.

"Traumatic Brain Injury: Hope Through Research | National Institute Of Neurological Disorders And Stroke". 2019. Ninds.Nih.Gov.

"Twitter". 2019. Twitter.Com.

"UCI Study Shows In-Home Therapy Effective For Stroke Rehabilitation". 2019. UCI News.

Wang, Guijing, Zefeng Zhang, Carma Ayala, Diane O. Dunet, Jing Fang, and Mary G. George. 2014. "Costs Of Hospitalization For Stroke Patients Aged 18-64 Years In The United States". Journal Of Stroke And Cerebrovascular Diseases 23 (5): 861-868. doi:10.1016/j.jstrokecerebrovasdis.2013.07.017.

"Ways To Give - National Brain Tumor Society". 2019. National Brain Tumor Society.

"What Is CTE?". 2019. Concussion Legacy Foundation.

"What Is Executive Function? How Executive Functioning Skills Affect Early Development". 2019. Center On The Developing Child at Harvard University.

"Who Will Keep The Public Healthy?: Educating Public Health Professionals For The 21St Century". 2004. Choice Reviews Online 41 (05): 41-2850-41-2850. doi:10.5860/choice.41-2850.

"Workplace Wellness Programs Fail To Improve Health, Study Finds". 2019. University Of Chicago News.

"Xconomy: The Decade Of The Brain: 25 Years Later". 2019. Xconomy.